THE THEORY OF
FLIGHT

The Theory of Flight

For the Layman

COLIN HOLCOMBE

Colin Holcombe

Acknowledgements

In researching information for this book, I am grateful to the following individuals, organisations, institutions and publications.

Flight: R. C. Grant.
Flight Without Formulae: A. C. Kermode
Gliding. A Handbook on Soaring Flight: Derek Piggott
Aerospace Museum Bristol
David Bradley, formerly of Airbus
Alan Roberts CEng FRAeS Aerodynamicist
Graham Clark, former Rolls-Royce project manager.
Royal Aeronautical Society
Chard Museum
Otto-Lilienthal-Museum
National Aeronautics and Space Administration (NASA)
I should like to give special thanks to Darren Harbar for his wonderful photography.

I should like to dedicate this book to David Bradley and the rest of the restoration team at Bristol Aerospace Museum and to all those dedicated volunteers around the country who give up much of their precious time to locate, save and restore historic aircraft. Without them, many examples of our rich aviation history would be lost for ever.

Contents

introduction

Introduction

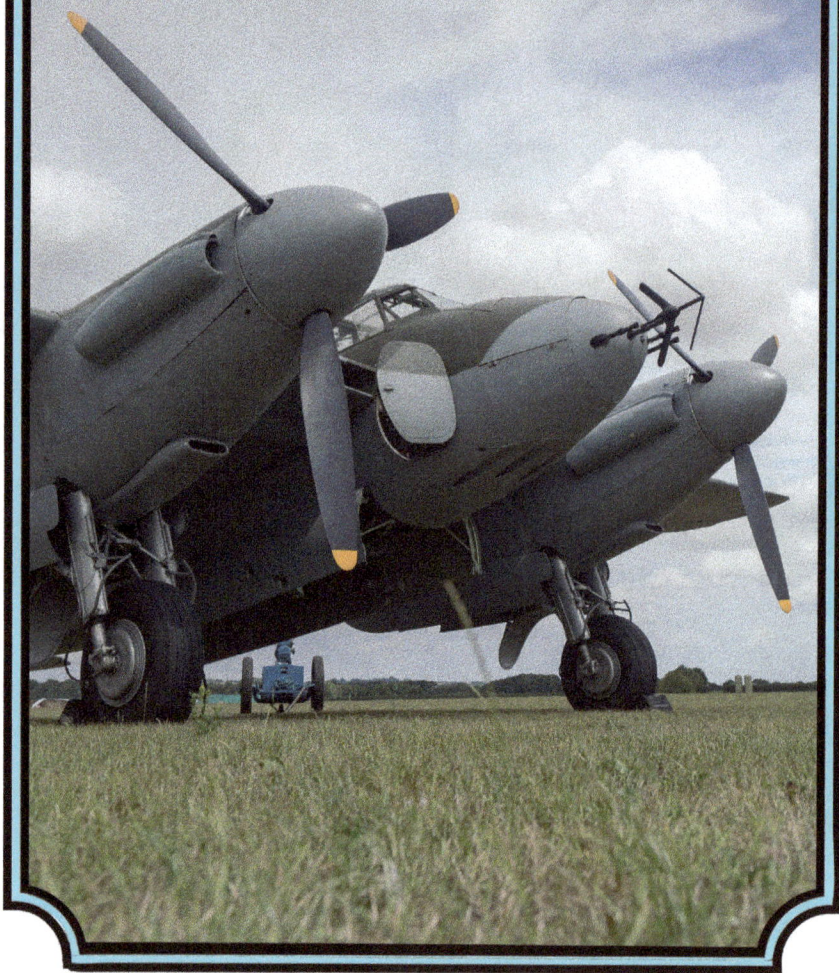

Darren Harbar Photography

INTRODUCTION

If you want to learn to fly an aeroplane you will need to have practical lessons from an instructor. This book will be of interest to you and helpful in understanding exactly what happens when you move the controls of your aircraft but it's not about how to fly an aircraft, it's about how an aircraft is able to fly. Why it is that if you push an aerofoil forward through the air it will experience two forces, lift and drag, and how those forces can be sufficient to lift a Boeing 747 or an Airbus A 380 full of hundreds of passengers and their luggage high into the air and carry them half way around the world.

I want to try and explain this incredible phenomenon in simple easy to understand terms as much as possible, even though that's not going to be easy when we have to talk about fluid dynamics, Bernoulli's theorem, Newton's third law, the Coanda effect and the like. But the truth is, I was never very good at maths and so I shall avoid the subject as much as possible. Although I used to fly gliders when I was younger and many of my friends and some of my family have worked in aviation, I have never done so myself. I learnt about how aircraft flies from talking to firstly, flying instructors when I was leaning to glide and then friends and family in the industry, so I'm a laymen myself and will explain how aircraft fly in laymens terms.

Back in 1916, no lesser person than Albert Einstein published a short article in a journal entitled, "Elementary Theory of Water Waves and Flight," the artical sort to explain the carrying capacity of the wings of flying machines. He even went so far as to design an aerofoil with a bulge on the top surface. The wing became known as the cat's-back wing because it resembled the back of a stretching cat. Luftverkehrsgesellschaft (LVG) in Berlin, built a new flying machine using Einstein's aerofoil, but a test pilot reported that the craft waddled around in the air like "a pregnant duck". Einstein much later referred to his attempts at aeronautical design as "youthful folly". So, if Einstein found designing aerofoils difficult what chance have mere mortals?

Some of man's great breakthroughs, inventions and discoveries have come because of the genius or insight of one or two men, but the theory of flight was the work of a great many men. Initially, the visionaries and romantics who just knew that one day man would fly, men like George Cayley, who first identified the four forces involved in heavier than air flight, Otto Lilienthal who eventually gave his life in the pursuit of flight and many more who built elaborate machines from wood and fabric and collected valuable data, including the Wright brothers who eventually achieved the first manned, heavier than air, powered flight. And of course, it didn't stop there. After the Wright brothers, others have increased man's knowledge to the extent that we can fly faster than the speed of sound and even land on the moon.

Growing up in central and North Bristol, I was exposed to aircraft and aeroplane manufacture from an early age, my father had spent the war on countless airfields around the country repairing Beaufighters and other aircraft, indeed the clock in our kitchen when I was growing up had once resided in just such a cockpit. At the age of ten we had just moved into a flat over my father's second hand furniture shop and it was around this time that I heard my first and only sonic-bang. I was outside the house, sorting out a tyre on my bike with my father, when we heard a loud double bang and the windows of our house shook. My father explained to me that we had just heard a plane going through the sound barrier, something that they wouldn't be allowed to do over a city now of course. I can only assume that something was being tested out of Filton aerodrome that was just a few miles away and home to Bristol Aeroplane Company (BAC) and Bristol Siddeley Engines (later Rolls-Royce,) easily Bristol's largest employers at the time.

Next door to us was a Green-grocer's shop and I became friendly with Alan Pegler, the son of the family who owned it and also lived over the shop. We became close friends and started senior school together in 1959. My bedroom at this time was filled with an array of both antique weaponry and models of aircraft, interspersed between the swords and muskets, I had everything from a Sopwith Pup to a Saturn Rocket and my friend Alan shared my interest in all things aviation.

We didn't think back then about how the aircraft flew, just how they were used and how cool they all were in their own ways. It was inevitable I suppose, that we would one day think about becoming pilots ourselves and when we were seventeen, we booked a week's gliding holiday at Nympsfield in Gloucestershire. We were both hooked and joined the club straight after.

It was for gliding that I had to learn the rudimentary physics of flight. It was necessary to know, not just in what way the various control surfaces controlled the attitude of the aircraft, but why they had that particular effect and I was fortunate enough to have instructors who would take the time to explain things to me in simple terms, unlike most of the books I looked at, that seemed to be full of mathematics, geometry and formula.

That's what I want to do here, write the book that I would have wanted back then, a book that would both explain to me in simple terms how an aeroplane can fly.

Some time ago, I was watching a news item on the television about some fashion models who were being flown off to an exotic destination to be photographed in the latest fashions. For some reason there was a large crowd seeing them off and they were being treated like celebrities, which I suppose they were. As I watched one of them turned to wave at the crowd as they stepped through the door of the aircraft that was going to whisk them away and I remember thinking, why are people so enthralled with them? They're only going to have their pictures taken somewhere, that's not so difficult, why are we not celebrating the men and women who designed the incredible feat of engineering that was going to get them there, surly those people are much more worthy of our adoration?

The technology that goes int making a modern jet aeroplane is something truly amazing. When you start to think about the design of a modern aerofoil or the onboard avionics it's mind bending enough, but then, when you think that some of the components in the engine are operating in temperatures well above their melting point, it becomes like science fiction

Now OK, before I get lots of protests from celebrities or those in the fashion industry, I have to confess that as a young lad, even I would have been far more likely to have a picture of Bridget Bardot or Sophia Loren on my wall, than I would of Barnes Wallis or Frank Whittle, sorry chaps!

Waiting for my first solo take-off in 1966, when I had lots of hair!

What is an Aeroplane?

Chapter 1

What is an Aeroplane?

If we're going to start at the very beginning, then I suppose we should first be clear about what we mean by aeroplane or aircraft. Well, any man-made structure which is capable of flight is an aircraft, but this is a very general term and will include balloons, airships, kites and helicopters as well as aeroplanes, which can themselves be of various different forms, such as gliders, seaplanes, flying boats, sailplanes and so on. I may be overcomplicating things a little early, so let's start by just saying that there are two types of aircraft, those which are lighter than air and those which are heavier than air, Fig 1.

We are not really concerned with lighter than air craft in this book but rather than just dismiss them out of hand, let's have a brief look at what they are and how they fly.

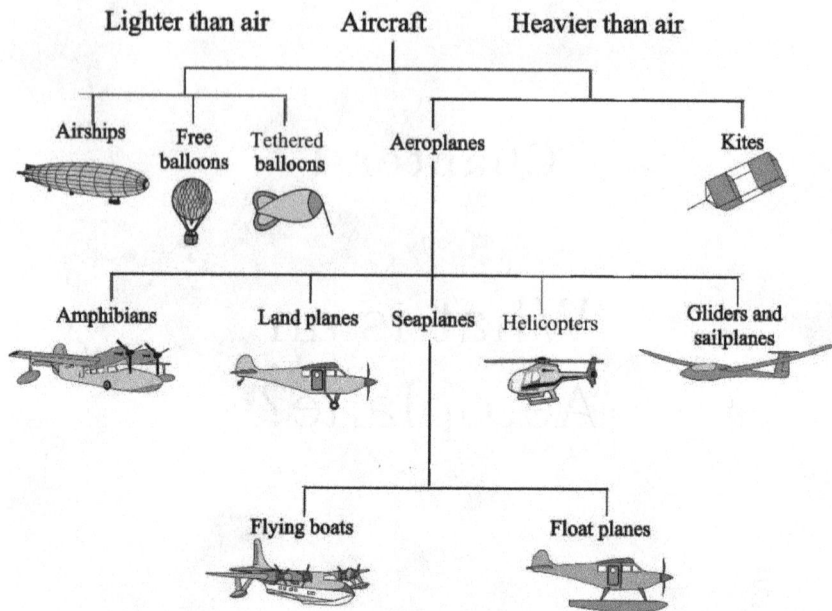

Fig 1

Lighter than Air

Everybody who went to school would have been taught, I hope, about the "Archimedes Principle," this states that when a body is immersed in a fluid, a force acts upwards upon it, helping to support its weight and that the upward force is equal to the weight of the fluid which is displaced by the body.

It may be easier to get your head around it by thinking about how a ship floats on water, water being an easier medium to visualise than air. When the hull of the ship enters the water, it displaces some of that water, and once it has displaced a volume of water that is equal in weight to the total weight of the ship, the ship will float, because the upward pressure will be enough to support it, Fig 2.

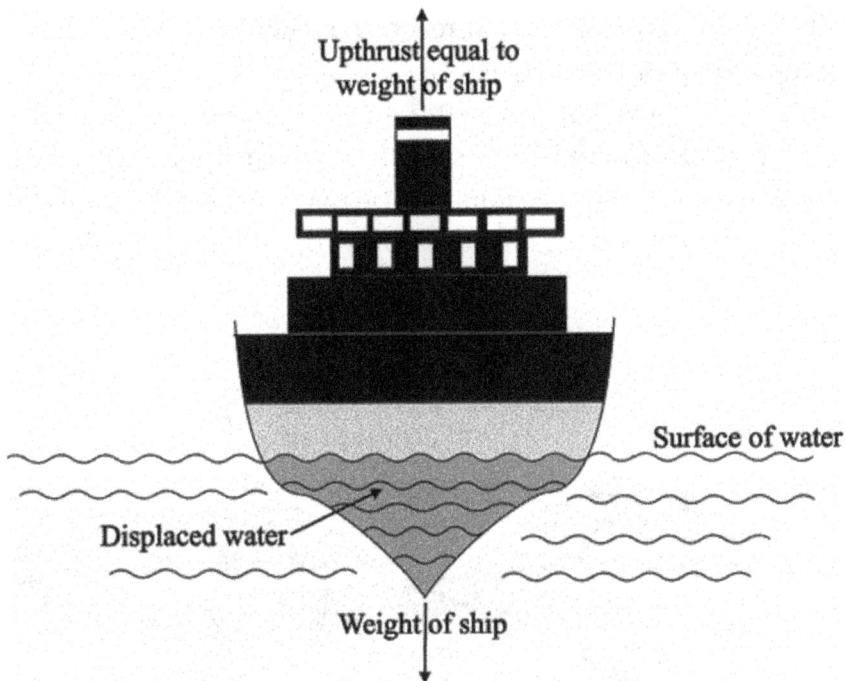

Fig 2

Now a fluid can be water or a gas, like air, and although the ship shown in Fig 2 is only partially immersed, the same principal applies to bodies that are totally immersed in the fluid. It is even true for bodies that don't float. If you were to weigh a lump of gold or lead in water, it will weigh less than if you weighed in the air, and the difference in the weight is exactly equal to the weight of the water that is displaced.

Now an airship or a balloon obtains its lift in exactly the same way as a ship. The envelope of the balloon displaces some air and therefore there is an upward force acting on the balloon which is equal to the weight of the displaced air. If the weight of the displaced air is equal to the weight of the balloon, the balloon will float in the air, if the weight of the displaced air is greater than the weight of the balloon, the balloon

will rise up in the air until it reaches a height where it is equal
to the weight of the displaced air.

Air does not weigh very much, so you can see why the envelope of the airship or balloon has to be so big, it has to displace
a large quantity of air to equal its own weight, Fig 3. The R100
and R101 each had a capacity of over five million cubic feet.

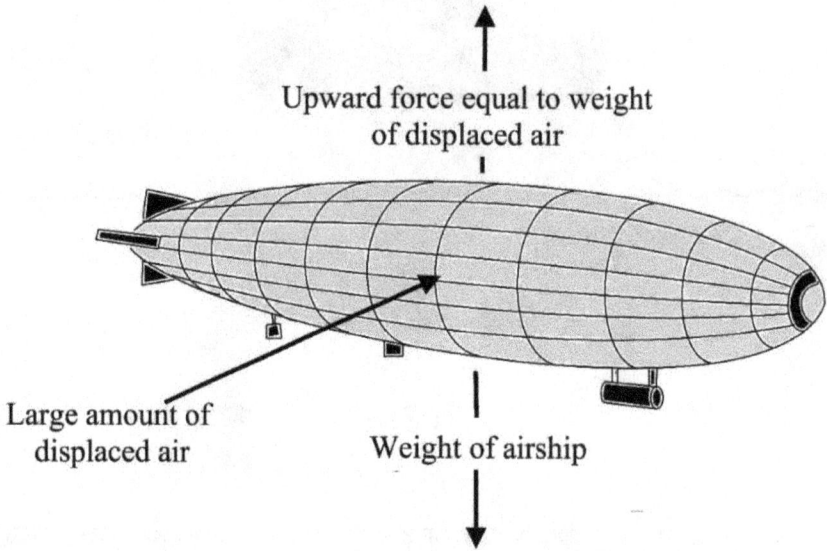

Upward force equal to weight
of displaced air

Large amount of
displaced air

Weight of airship

Fig 3

One of the biggest problems with airships is the fact that,
as you ascend through the atmosphere, the air becomes thinner and therefore weighs less than it did nearer the ground.
This means that as the airship or balloon gains height, the air
that it displaces weighs less and will therefor support less, if
for instance, an airship only just floats in the air when it's near
the ground, it will not be able to do so higher up because the
weight of the thinner air will not be sufficient to support it, it
will therefore not be able to rise. This is the reason why airships carry ballast, additional weight that can be jettisoned to
lighten the weight of the airship. Obviously when you wish to

descend, you cannot add weight, so the only thing you can do is let out some of the gas and either allow air to take its place or the envelope to decrease in size, displacing less air.

The other problem with airships, is the difficulty of stabilising the interior and exterior pressure as the envelope ascends through thinning air and this is the reason weather balloons, that reach great height, are so tall and thin when on the ground, allowing for considerable expansion as they rise up through the thinning atmosphere.

Hot-air balloons

Hot air rises because it is less dense than cold air and therefore weighs less, so hot-air balloons fly using exactly the same principal, the less dense and therefore lighter hot air inside the balloon, displacing the heavier cold air around it.

The Atmosphere

Chapter 2

The Atmosphere

Now that we know what an aeroplane is, we need to know something of the medium in which it flies, the air or atmosphere. The main features of the air that concern us when attempting to fly, are its density and weight and its temperature, all of which fall off with increases in height and Fig 4 gives you some idea of these changes.

Height	Temp.	Pressure	Weight of 100 cubic ft. Of air
60,000 ft.	-57^0	1 Lb per Square inch	1 Lb
40,000 ft.	-57^0	3 Lb per Square inch	2 Lb
20,000 ft.	-25^0	7 Lb per Square inch	4 Lb
Sea Level	$+15^0$	15 Lb per Square inch	8 Lb

Fig 4 Measurements will vary day to day according to prevailing conditions

The reason the air pressure is greater per square inch at sea level than it is at height, is because it has to support the weight of the air above it, at sea level there a lot of air above it to be supported, at higher altitudes there is not so much. This is also the reason it increases in density and weight the lower you are, the more weight of air above it, the denser it becomes. The temperature of the air also falls off with height, but not in quite such a straight forward uniform way. Up to approximately 36,000 ft. above sea level, the fall-off in temperature is quite regular, about 2 degrees centigrade per thousand feet of rise but after that the temperature remains fairly constant at about minus 57 degrees centigrade.

The lower part of the atmosphere, where the temperature drops off, is called the troposphere and the higher part, where the temperature is more constant, is called the stratosphere, the surface dividing the two is known as the tropopause.

The most annoying thing about the atmosphere, ask any Englishman, is its changeability. It's a fluid resting on the surface of a rotating sphere that has an uneven surface and is continually being heated by the sun one minute but not the next, so the atmosphere itself is constantly in motion. Pick any spot on the earth and the atmospheric conditions there are going to change, not just day to day, but hour by hour, even minute by minute.

Air moves around for a variety of reasons, it is constantly being heated up and cooled down by the sun as the earth rotates and will naturally migrate from areas of high pressure to areas of low pressure, causing winds. All of this movement and changeability has meant that we have had to adopt an average set of conditions called the, "International Standard Atmosphere." Now there may never be a day, anywhere, where these conditions exist exactly all the way up, but they serve as a standard by which we can compare the performance of aircraft. When an attempt is made, for instance, to set a new height record, the height allowed is not the actual height achieved, but the height which, according to calculation, would have been achieved if the conditions had been the same as the International Standard Atmosphere.

Wind

Now the first part of this book is about how an aeroplane flies, it's not about how to fly an aeroplane, so you don't need to know a lot of detail about weather conditions but as this chapter is about the atmosphere, some explanation of air movement seems appropriate.

You will read later that we live at the bottom of an approximately 200 mile deep ocean of air and that the air pressure at sea level is around 15lb. per square inch, meaning that the column of air sitting atop each square inch space weighs 15lb. Now the air is being warmed by the sun and the earth is rotating, so the air is constantly moving and the exact height of the atmosphere varies from place to place and time to time. The air pressure is measured in millibars and the average pressure at sea level is 1013.25 millibars.

Naturally the air will tend to move from areas of high pressure to areas of low pressure, Fig 5.

Millibars

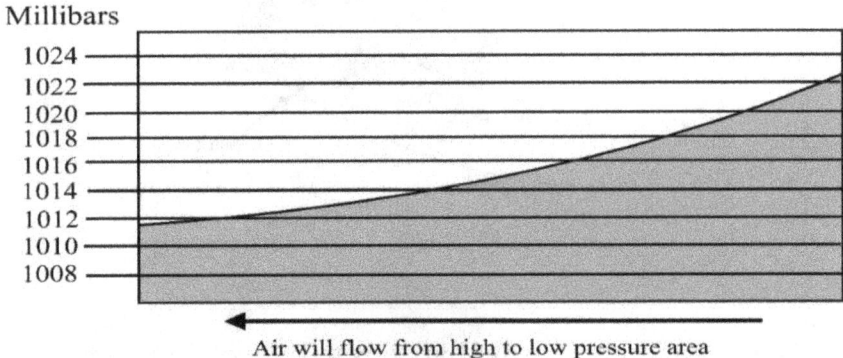

Air will flow from high to low pressure area

Fig 5

Now let's follow a column of air, say one on our pressure map marked as a red square, Fig 6, that is just south of Portsmouth on an isobar marked as 1018 millibars. An isobar is a line on a weather map connecting areas of equal pressure. This column of air will start to move from its present position, where the pressure is 1018mbs, in a North Westerly direction towards Bath at right angles to the isobars, but things are not as simple as they appear at first, because the earth is rotating.

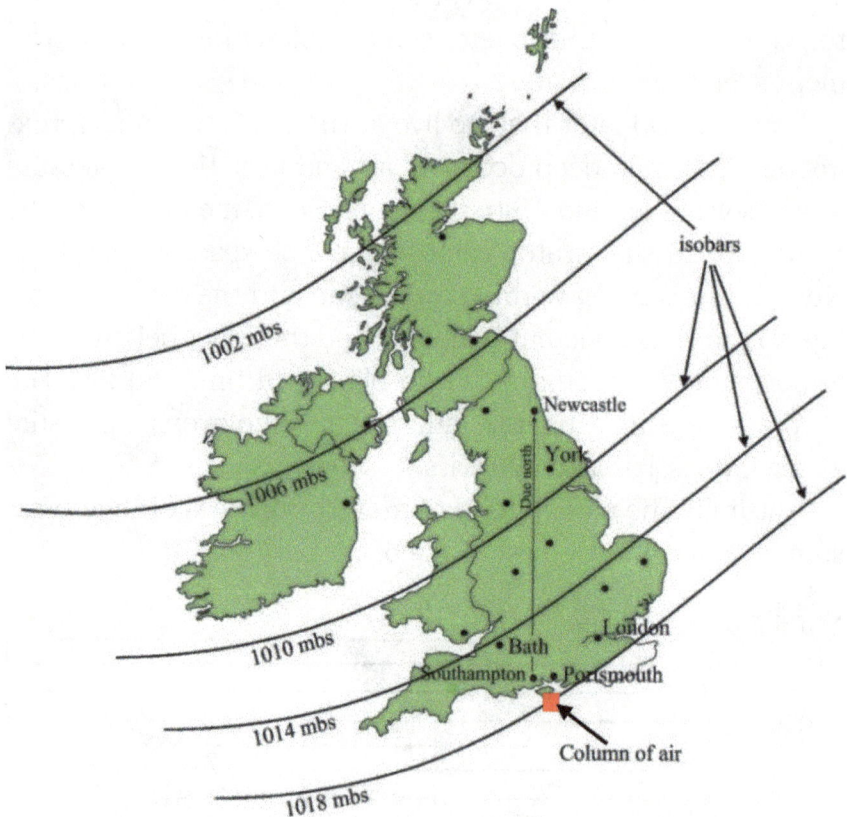

isobars

1002 mbs

Newcastle

York

Due north

1006 mbs

London

1010 mbs

Bath

Southampton   Portsmouth

1014 mbs

Column of air

1018 mbs

Fig 6

The explanation of what happens to our column of air may be easier to understand if we first look at a simple, though by no means complete analogy. Imagine, as I often do, that you are the world's greatest golfer, who always, without exception, hits his ball straight up the fairway in a perfectly straight line every time. Now imaging that you are capable of hitting a golf ball all the way from Southampton to Newcastle due north. We'll stretch our imagination a little further and say that you can quite clearly see the flag on the green there. You line yourself up to hit your ball on a direct line from your tee in Southampton to the flag in Newcastle, and as always, you hit the perfect shot. When you see your ball start off you are very pleased but this soon turns to disbelief as some mysterious force drags your ball off course and it drops into the North Sea.

Actually, there is nothing mysterious about it, you simply forgot that the earth is rotating, giving you and everything with you at 51° North, the latitude of Southampton, a speed of 567 knots in an easterly direction, even your golf ball has that velocity as you hit it. Newcastle on the other hand, has a latitude of 55° North, giving it an easterly speed of only 516 knots, meaning it lags behind in the easterly rush through space. Now what you've witnessed looks so much as if some mysterious force has acted on your ball that it is actually called the "Geostrophic Force."

This Geostrophic force has three definite characteristics:

1. In the northern hemisphere the force acts on air moving over the earth's surface to the right of the direction of movement. In the Southern hemisphere the force acts towards the left of the direction of movement.

2. The magnitude of the force is proportional to the speed of the air, so the faster the air is moving, the stronger the force.

3. The magnitude of the force varies with latitude; it increases from zero at the Equator to a maximum at the poles.

Now let us return to the parcel of air south of Portsmouth on the 1018 isobar. It will begin its journey heading north west towards Bath. However, just as our golf ball was pulled off course to the right, so will our parcel of air.

As the air begins to move it is pulled to the right by the geostrophic force, and this continues until the air is moving parallel to the isobars, see Fig 7.

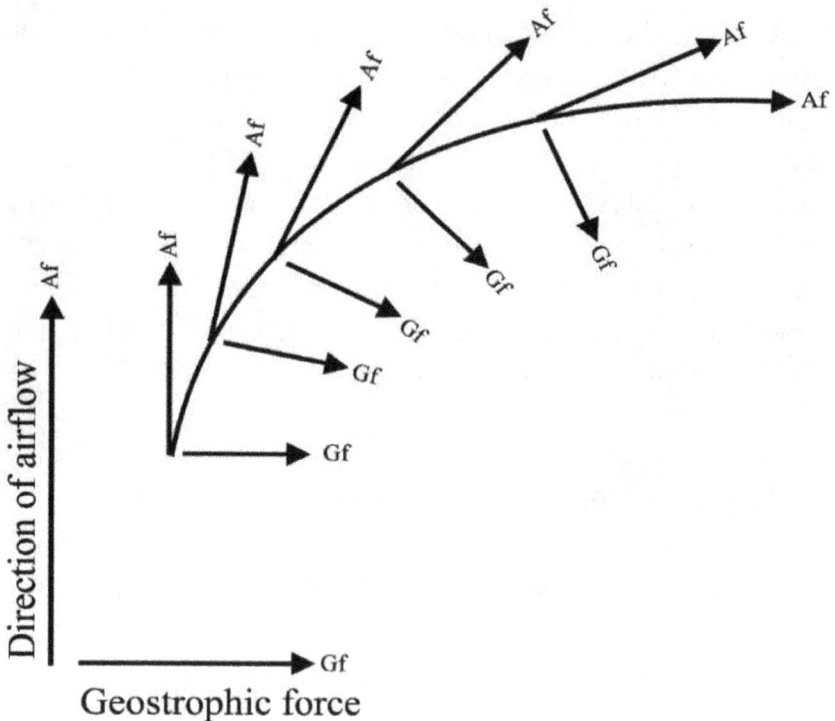

Fig 7 As the air travels it is pulled to the right by the geostopic force

At this stage the geostrophic force is exactly equal in magnitude and opposite in direction to the pressure gradient force, which has remained unchanged. This balance of the two forces will be preserved as long as the air flows parallel to the isobars with just sufficient speed for the pressure gradient and geostrophic forces to balance each other.

Any deviation can only be temporary as the geostrophic force would soon redress the balance.

The wind speed necessary to maintain the balance is determined by the steepness of the pressure gradient, Fig 8. If the pressure gradient B is double that of A then the geostrophic force must be double. Airflow is affected by other factors as well but they are minor in comparism and of little interest to us here.

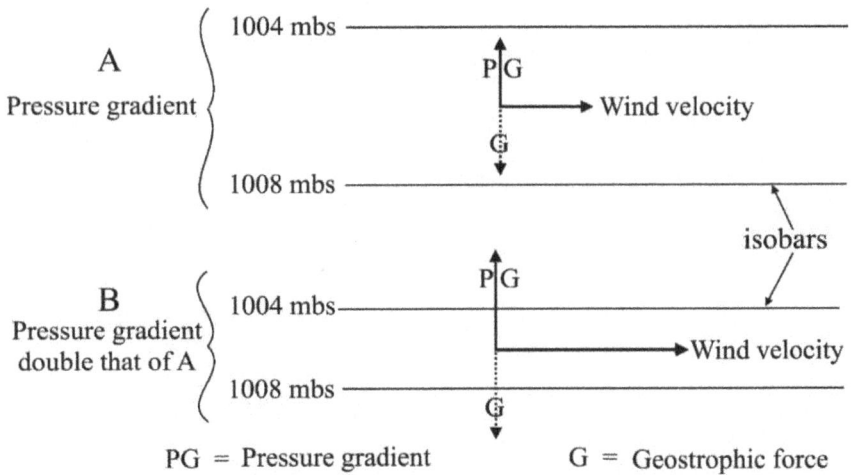

PG = Pressure gradient   G = Geostrophic force

Fig 8 If the pressure gradient PG is double, the geostropic force must be double for balance and this is attained when the wind speed is doubled.

Space

The natural next question is I suppose, what happens when you go up beyond the atmosphere? Well here again, as with lighter than air aircraft, it is not something that this book is really concerned with because missiles, satellites and space-craft are not aircraft according to our definition, but let's just have a brief look at them here and get them out of the way.

Let's start by looking at the most familiar missile, a ball, let's say a cricket ball. If you throw the ball vertically up, it will travel to a certain height, gradually slowing in upward veloc-ity as gravity pulls on it, until it comes to a stop and begins falling back to earth, all very straightforward. But what hap-pens if you throw the ball horizontal to the ground? Well as soon as the ball is released from your hand, the force of gravity will begin to pull it down to the ground, tracing a path some-thing like the ones shown in Fig 9.

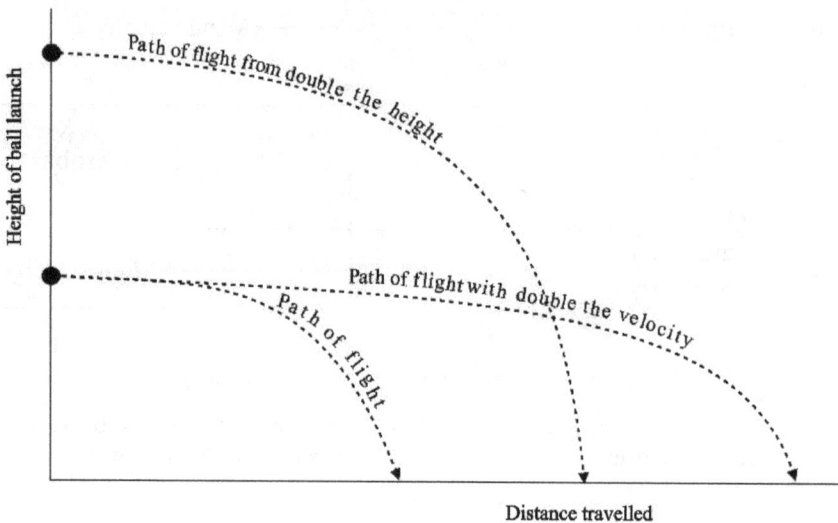

Fig 9

This assumes that the earth is flat and that the ball is launched exactly parallel to the ground. It is clear that the distance the ball travels is dependent upon both the height from which it was launched and the velocity with which it was projected, it is also clear that it will hit the ground somewhere eventually if the ground is flat. However, the earth is not flat, it is curving downwards away from you. Now that may not make a lot of difference over the sort of distance you can throw a cricket ball, or even the distance a bullet will travel from a gun, but if you think about the sort of speeds we can obtain now and you launch your missile from some height, it makes a great deal of difference and the curvature of the earth becomes a major factor.

Someone once asked me, and it was someone who should have known better, how it was that the astronauts in the international space station are said to be in zero gravity and weightless, when the space station itself is being held in orbit by the earth's gravity?

Well the answer is quite simple, both the international space station and the brave men and women in it, are both in the grip of earth's gravity and are in fact falling to the ground at the same rate as each other, however, they, just like our cricket ball, also have forward velocity, and that velocity and the height above the ground they are, means that they are always falling to earth beyond the horizon, Fig 10.

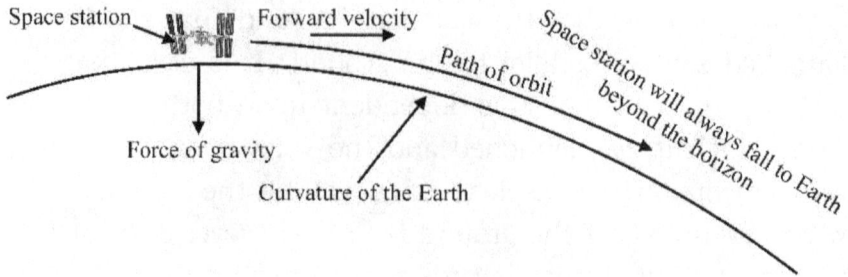

Fig 10. The forward velocity is enough to ensure that the space station will always be falling to earth beyond the horizon, putting it into an orbit around the earth.

Astronauts are given a taste of weightless conditions in what has become known as the "vomit comet" owing to the number of people who are actually sick during the experience.

A specially fitted out airliner takes them up to a height where the aircraft follows a parabolic flight path relative to the centre of the earth. Initially the aircraft climbs with a pitch angle of 45 degrees using engine thrust and elevator controls. The sensation of weightlessness is then achieved by reducing thrust and lowering the nose to maintain a neutral or "zero lift" configuration such that the aircraft follows a ballistic trajectory, with the engine thrust exactly compensating for drag.

Weightlessness begins while ascending and lasts all the way up-and-over the hump, until the aircraft reaches a downward pitch angle of around 30 degrees. At this point the aircraft is pointing downwards at high speed and must begin to pull back into another nose-up attitude to repeat the manoeuvre. The forces are roughly twice that of gravity on the way down, at the bottom and starting up again. This lasts all the way until the aircraft is again halfway up its upward trajectory, when the pilot again reduces thrust and lowers the nose, Fig 10a. The experience is similar to that of traveling at speed over a hump-back bridge.

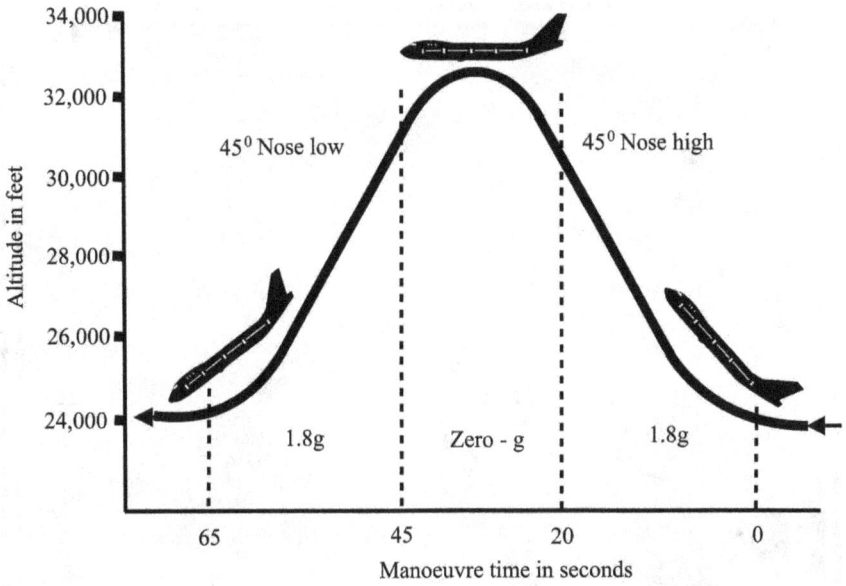

Fig 10A. Parabolic flight path

Lift and Drag

Chapter 3

Lift and Drag

Lift and Drag

Let's now return to our main topic, aeroplanes and how they fly. We've looked at what an aircraft actually is and the medium in which it flies, so let's now look at two of the main forces that act on it in flight, lift and drag.

We know that in order for an aircraft to fly we have to provide it with a lifting force that is at least equal to its weight. In lighter than air aircraft this lifting force was provided by the displacement of air, but with heavier than air craft it is provided in an entirely different way.

What happens if you take a stiff piece of cardboard and push it through the air with its front, or leading edge, inclined up slightly, being a little higher than the back, or trailing edge? You will feel a force acting on it, pushing it up and backwards, the same, but not as obvious as if you were pushing it through water. The upward part of that force is called, *lift,* and the backward part of the force is called *drag,* Fig 11.

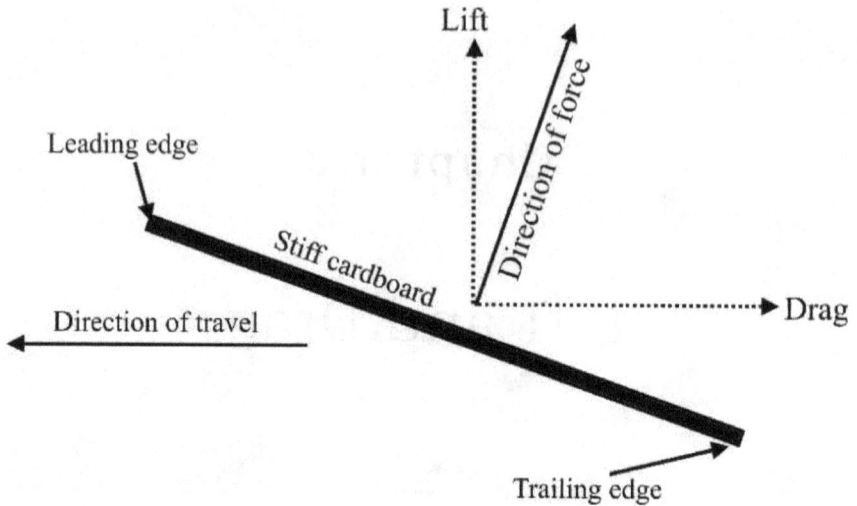

Fig 11 The two forces of lift and drag

Now that, in the very basic of terms, is how an aeroplane flies. The piece of cardboard is acting exactly like the wing of an aeroplane. Of course, getting an aeroplane to fly is a lot more complicated than that, but it is the basic principle.

Now the angle created when we lift the leading edge is called "the angle of attack" and we will refer to it quite a bit, so let's be clear what is meant by it. You've probably worked it out for yourselves, as it is quite easy to see when we are talking about a piece of stiff cardboard, but soon we will be looking at wings with curved surfaces and then it is not so easy, because with curved surfaces there is no straight line to take our angle from, we will have to add one, and it will vary in position depending on the shape of the wing.

Fig 12, shows where this datum or chord line is drawn on different wings.

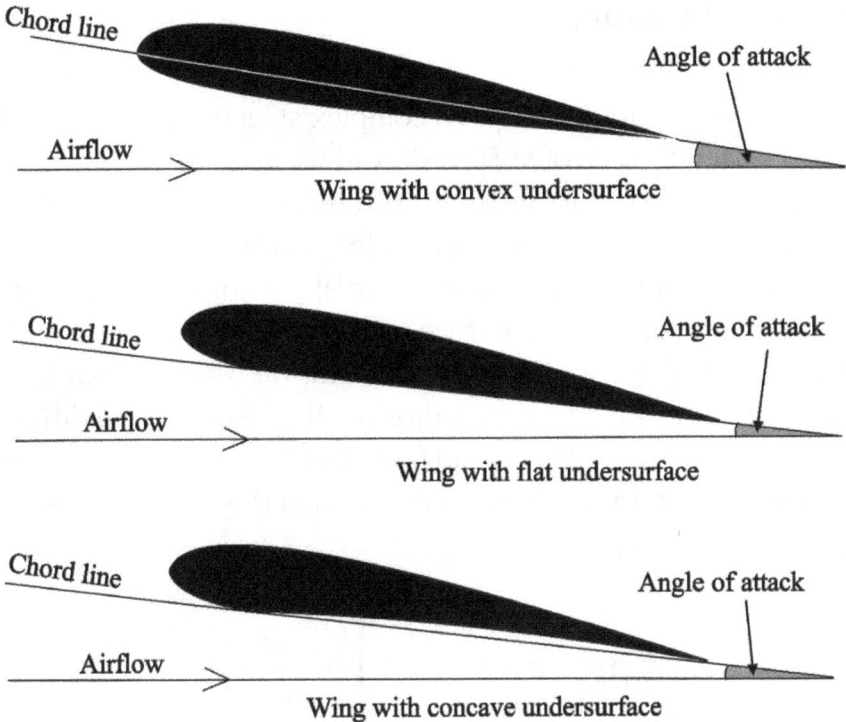

Fig 12. The angle of attack

The trouble we have is that, if you let go of the cardboard as it is traveling forward, the force will most probably flip it over on its back, not very comfortable and I would imagine quite frightening for any passengers, so in order to maintain the lift, we have to constantly provide the forward motion or "thrust."

It's important to remember, however, that the forward motion is through the air, it doesn't have to be motion over the ground. A kite flies even though it has no forward motion over the ground, but it is moving forward in relation to the air as the wind blows over it. The same is true for our cardboard wing, it makes no difference whether it is the wing moving through the air or the air moving over the wing, the effect is the same. In practice it is normally a combination of the two.

Centre of Pressure

A modern aircraft wing is a complex structure, so I want to stick with our piece of stiff cardboard for a moment longer.

If, as we push our cardboard through the air, we hold it at the centre of each end, we feel the forward and backward force acting on it but it will tend to rotate. If we hold it further forward of the centre line, or if we add weights to it there so that the centre of gravity is further forward, we will find that it is the back or trailing edge that flips up. If we keep trying different points on the sides to hold it, we will eventually find a spot where it doesn't try to flip either way, and that is the centre of pressure, Fig 13.

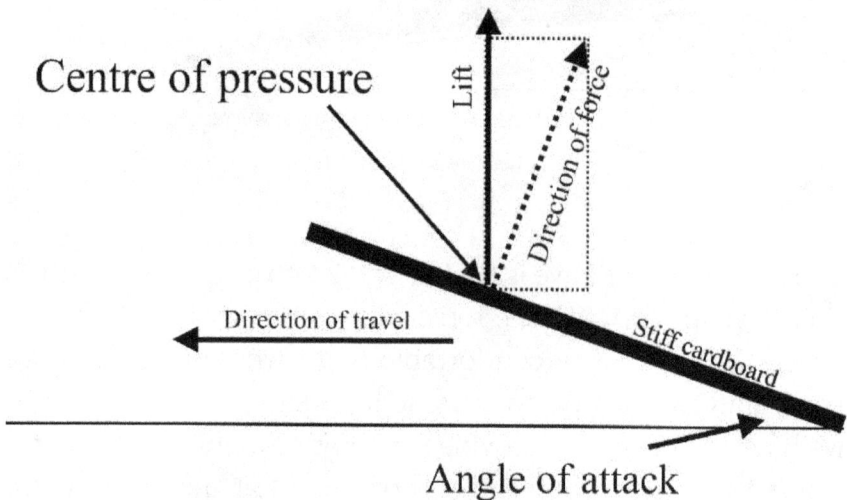

Fig 13. Centre of pressure

Stability

When the centre of pressure and the centre of gravity are at the same spot the wing is balanced or is said to be in equilibrium. If the centre of pressure is in front of the centre of gravity the wing is said to be *tail-heavy*, whereas if the centre of pressure is behind the centre of gravity it is said to be *nose-heavy*, Fig 14.

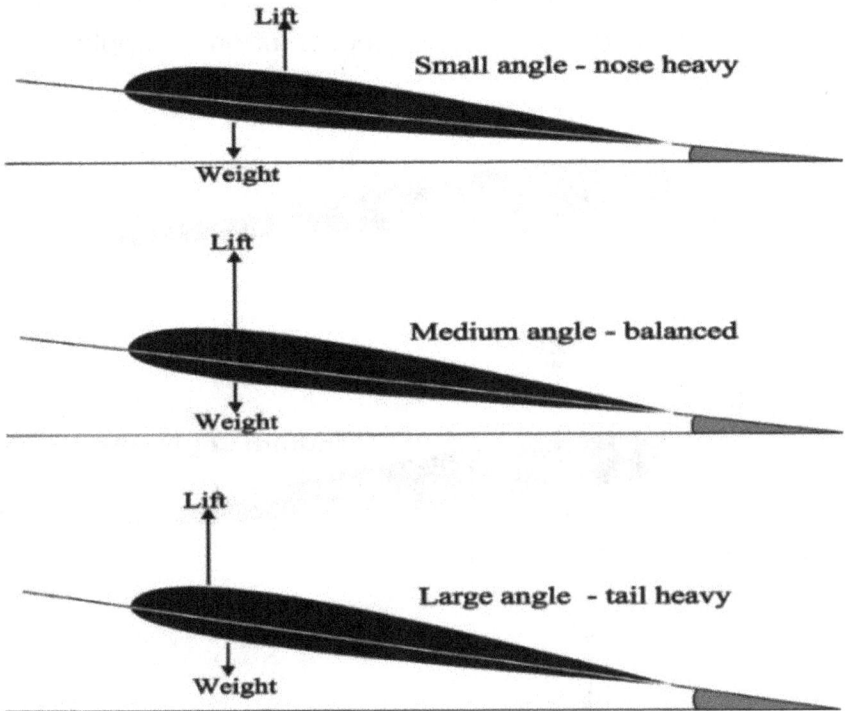

Fig 14

Now the centre of pressure doesn't always stay in the same place, it moves as you alter the angle of attack. If, as we lift the leading edge, increasing the angle of attack, the centre of pressure moves forward so that it is in front of the centre of gravity, this will tend to push the leading edge further up, increasing the angle still more and so moving the centre of pressure further forward and so on. This is called an "unstable state." The mere fact that things become bad makes them tend to become worse.

If, however, the centre of pressure moves backwards with an increase in the angle of attack, it will be behind the centre of gravity and will tend to push the leading edge down again and restore the original angle. This is called a "stable state," when things become bad, influences tend to make them better, Fig 15. So, you can see that if you want your aeroplane to be stable you have to arrange for the latter conditions to apply.

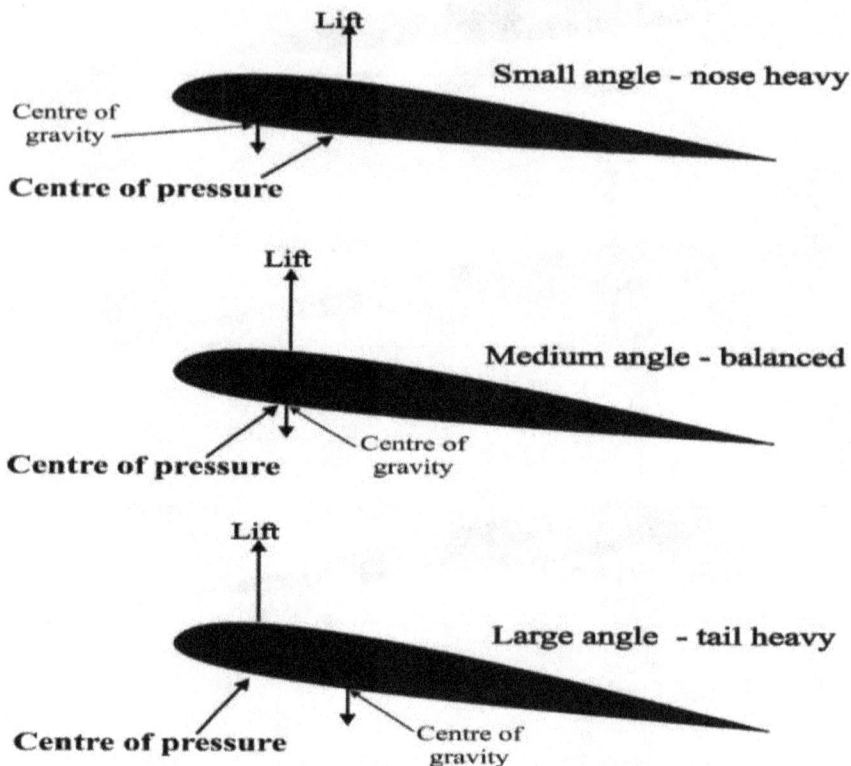

Fig 15 Top illustration stable Bottom illustration unstable

The Wing Section

Hands up, all those who have seen an aeroplane standing on the runway ready to take off, that had wings shaped like a piece of stiff cardboard? I thought not, so let's now have a look at a true aerofoil or wing section. In reality a wing section is made up of two differently curved surfaces, the name for which is an aerofoil, but I prefer, and will continue to refer to it as a wing.

The reason for employing curved surfaces is that we need some thickness to give the wing some strength and curved surfaces supply much better lift, for reasons we will look at in detail soon, but this may be a good time to explain what is known as the Coandă effect, named after Henri Coandă, a Romanian aerodynamics pioneer and inventor who built experimental aircraft.

The Coandă effect is the tendency for a stream or jet of fluid to stay attached to or follow a convex surface. It is described by Henri Coandă himself as "*the tendency of a jet of fluid emerging from an orifice to follow an adjacent flat or curved surface and to entrain fluid from the surroundings so that a region of lower pressure develops.*"

Coandă was the first to recognize the practical application of the phenomenon in aircraft design and if you need confirmation of the effect yourself, just turn on a kitchen tap and hold the back of a spoon bowl against the stream of water to see the stream follow the surface of the spoon, Fig 16.

Fig 16 The Coandă effect

Sir Isaac Newton said that, "To every action there is an equal and opposite reaction." Therefore, the greater the amount of air pushed down by our wing the greater will be pressure or lift pushing up, but on the other hand, the greater the disturbance caused to the air as the wing is pushed through it, the greater will be the resistance or drag.

The downward flow of air leaving an aircraft's wing is called the downwash, so when designing a wing and choosing an angle of attack, the idea is to secure as much lift and downwash as possible without causing eddies or disturbance that contribute towards drag. An eddy is the swirling of air and reverse current caused when a flow of air is disturbed or in a turbulent flow. This is why a curved surface is so much superior to a flat one, and why we use a only a small angle of attack. The gradual curvature of the surface directs the air downward and the Coandă effect prevents it from suddenly breaking away from the top surface and forming eddies, Fig 16A. A larger angle of attack would give more lift but it would also cause more disturbance and eddies.

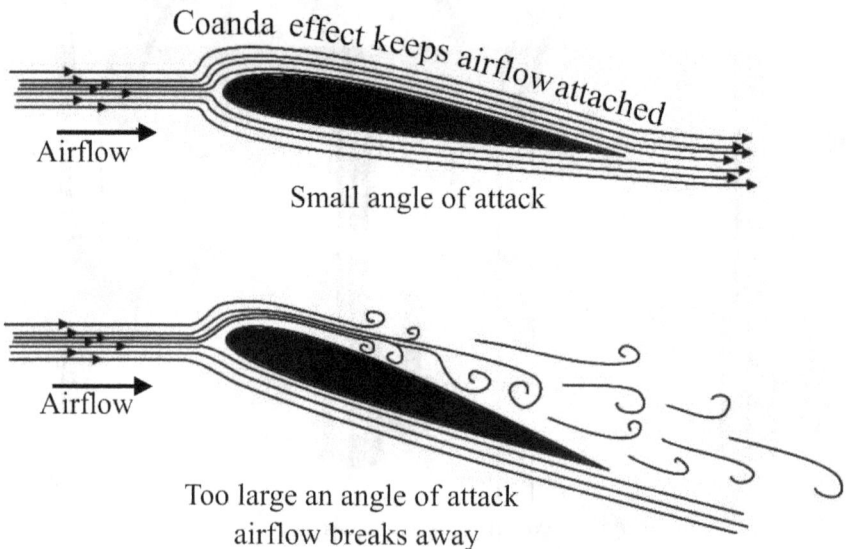

Coanda effect keeps airflow attached

Airflow

Small angle of attack

Airflow

Too large an angle of attack
airflow breaks away

Fig 16A A . small angle of attack is needed to prevent too much disturbance

Air Pressure

We live at the bottom of a vast ocean of air that is around 200 miles deep and although air is quite light it does have weight and at low levels the air is compressed by the weight of the air above it. If you refer back to Fig 3 you will see that, at sea level it is around 15 lb. per square inch, or about one kilogram per square centimetre. This is called the atmospheric pressure, or sometimes the barometric pressure, "baros" being the Greek word for weight and it is measured with a barometer, Fig 17.

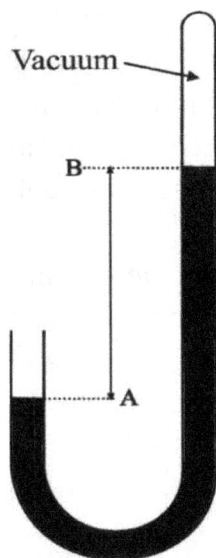

Fig 17 A Mercury Barometer

The mercury barometer is just a form of balance, the weight of the air resting on the surface at A, exactly balances the weight of the mercury in the tube between A and B, the space above B being a vacuum.

We saw earlier that the pressure on the inclined wing was upwards and backward, (Lift and Drag) and that we could locate a centre of pressure but that doesn't mean the pressure is only in one place on the wing, it is of course distributed over the whole surface, both above and below. Now this pressure, although distributed over the whole wing surface, is by no means distributed evenly when there is airflow over the wing, it varies from place to place. There is a way of plotting the variations in pressure over the wing surface which is employed by designers and aeronautical engineers, but it's very technical and we only need to know the results here, not the details of how the results are obtained. By using this process of "pressure plotting", it is possible to draw a detailed map, showing where the pressure is greater or smaller over the wing surface, but again, all we really need to know at the moment is that such maps show a general increase in pressure on the bottom surface and a decrease in pressure on the upper surface.

The increase in pressure on the bottom surface is due to the wing pressing the air down, remember, every action has an equal and opposite reaction. The decrease in pressure over the top surface is due to the fact that the airflow speeds up over the top of the wing.

Now you might think that the increase in pressure under the wing would be greater than the decrease in pressure above the wing but in fact the opposite is true! It is the top surface of the wing that contributes the larger proportion of the lift. It is also true that we obtain more lift from the front of the wing than the back, and so when we think of the force as acting in one place, the centre of pressure, we have to see it as being in front of the centre of gravity.

The points we are talking about at the moment are very important and we need to be clear that the differences in pressure are not huge differences, when the wing is at rest and there is no airflow over it, the pressure above and below are the same, around 15lb. per square inch. When there is airflow over the wing there is a slight increase in pressure below and just a slightly bigger decrease above.

Why draughts shut doors

You may feel that my simply stating that it is the act of the airflow following the upper curvature of the wing and speeding up that results in a decrease in pressure above the wing, doesn't really convince you of the fact, so we'll look at the effect in a bit more depth.

Let's consider water instead of air for a moment, because water is easier to visualise than air and both being fluids, they behave in much the same way.

Imagine a river flowing at a particular rate, meaning that a particular volume of water will pass a particular spot on the bank every minute. If you watch the top surface of the river it will appear to speed up and slow down in different sections and that is because the depth of the river varies. In general, where the river is deep, it doesn't have to flow as fast for the same volume of water to pass, Fig 18.

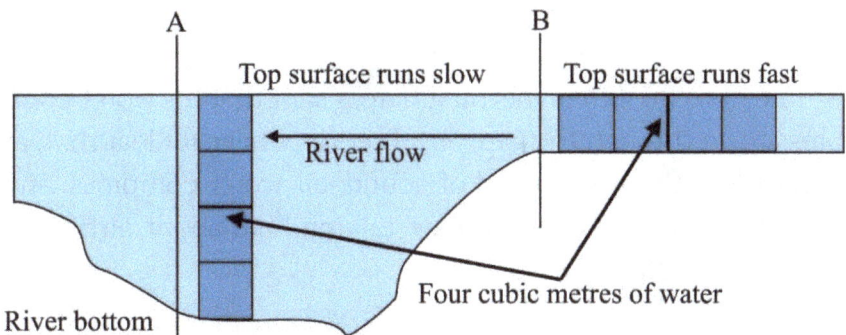

Fig 18 River runs slower for the four cubic metres to pass A but faster for the four metres to pass B

Now, imagine that the river, instead of varying in depth, is the same depth along its full length but gets narrower at some point. The same thing will happen, where the volume of water needs to get through the narrow part of the river the flow will speed up, rush through and then slow down again the other side, Fig 19. This is because the water won't compress to go through the narrow gap, so it needs to speed up, and air behaves in exactly the same way. If only cinema and theatre crowds would behave like air and water when leaving a performance, there would be no crush at the doors. If, when people stood up to leave, they started to walk slowly towards the exit doors and gradually increased their pace as they got nearer, walked quickly through the doors and then began to slow down again the other side, there would be no crush at the doors and everybody would get through without having to wait for anyone else.

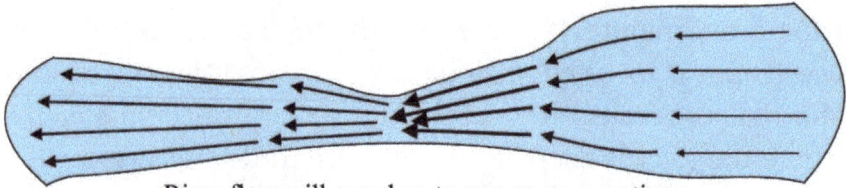

River flow will speed up to pass narrow section

Fig 19 River water will speed up to pass narrow section of river

I need to qualify something here, I said that air won't compress to go through the gap, now I need to make it clear that, at speeds less than the speed of sound, air won't compress, and for the moment at least, we are talking here about airflow at subsonic speeds.

The Venturi tube

Now we're going to stay with this phenomenon of pressure falling off with an increase in air speed a little longer because it is an important factor and it is not that intuitive. Venturi tubes, are basically tubes through which fluids are passed, that have a constriction or throat in them to increase the air speed and reduce pressure, and they are used in all sorts of devices.

Fig 20, shows air passing through a Venturi tube and speeding up to do so with its consequential drop in pressure.

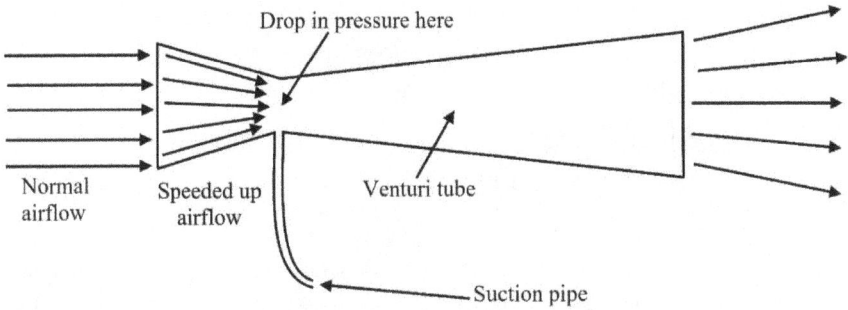

Drop in pressure here

Normal airflow

Speeded up airflow

Venturi tube

Suction pipe

Fig 20. A Venturi tube

A perfume *atomizer* for example, operates by having air forced from a squeeze-bulb, through a Venturi tube that reduces the pressure above an open suction pipe dipped into liquid perfume. The drop in atmospheric pressure in the venturi tube then draws the perfume up the suction pipe into the airstream, where the liquid is "atomized" into small droplets that are carried forward in a spray by the rapid flow of the air, Fig 21.

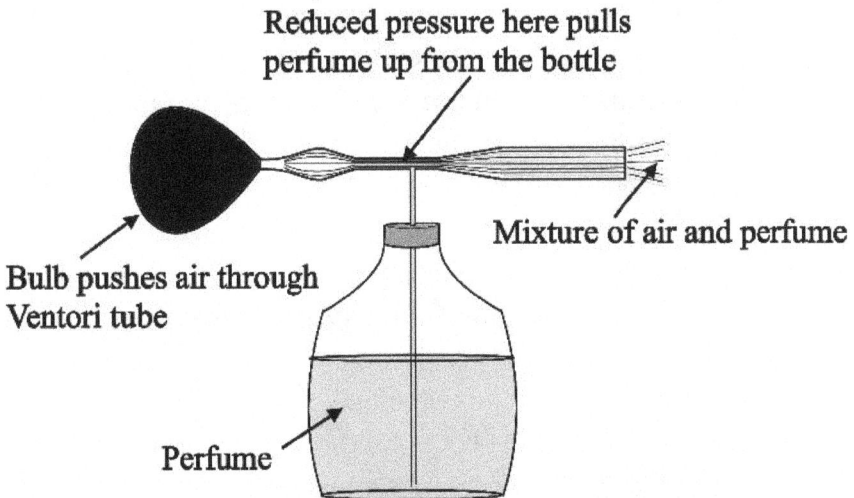

Reduced pressure here pulls perfume up from the bottle

Mixture of air and perfume

Bulb pushes air through Ventori tube

Perfume

Fig 21. Perfume atomizer utilising a venturi tube

OK you cry, so air speeds up to go through a gap, but why does this create a drop in air-pressure? Well the answer is something called "Bernoulli's Theorem," and it would be much easier if we just accepted it as a fact and moved on, but for those of you who insist on knowing, it is all to do with the conservation of energy.

A fluid can exert pressure for two reasons, firstly, because of any movement, such as when a wind blows in your face and secondly, because of the energy stored in it which makes it exert pressure on the sides of a vessel that contains it, such as the envelope of a balloon. The pressure due to movement is called dynamic pressure and the other is called static pressure.

Bernoulli's Theorem states that, in a steady flow, the sum of all forms of energy in a fluid along a streamline is the same at all points on that streamline. This requires that the sum of kinetic or dynamic energy, potential energy, and internal energy remains constant. Thus, an increase in the speed of the fluid, which results in an increase in its dynamic energy, also results in a simultaneous decrease in its static energy.

Things are however, not quite as easy as that because, the opposite is also true, not only does an increase in the velocity of airflow result in a drop in pressure, so a drop in pressure *can* also result in an increase in the velocity of the airflow.

In order for the airflow to stick to the top surface of the wing (Coanda effect), the pressure is reduced which gives the necessary centripetal acceleration to make the air follow the curved surface. The increased velocity is the result of this reduction in pressure which accelerates the flow because of the pressure difference over the curved part of the wing relative to the pressure at the leading edge. As the curve reduces towards the trailing edge the pressure increases again towards the ambient static pressure. At the trailing edge of a lifting wing the air comes off in a rearward and downward direction, (downwash). So, the wing has accelerated the air downwards with a force that is equal and opposite to the upward lift force on the wing.

Well, you asked for it!

Just remember that the airflow is separated by the leading edge and forced to travel either over the top or the bottom of the wing, Fig 22. The air traveling under the wing is entering an area of increased pressure and slows down slightly. The air traveling over the top of the wing is entering an area of reduced pressure and speeds up. Reduced pressure and increased velocity of airflow go together.

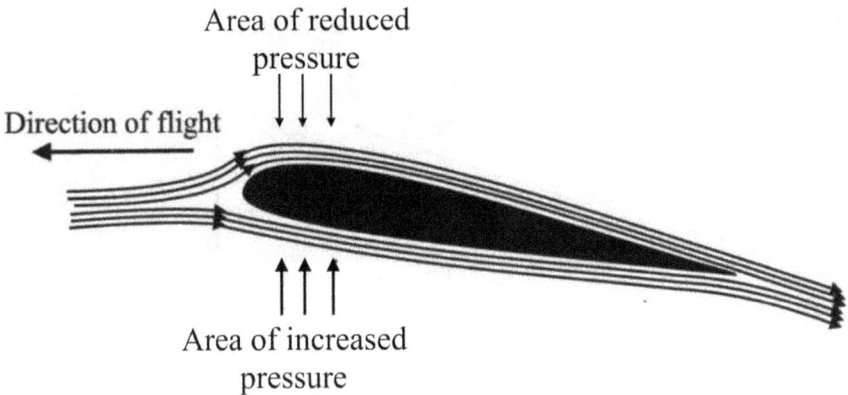

Area of reduced
pressure

Direction of flight

Area of increased
pressure

Fig 22

Now if you need further proof that a pressure drop and an increase in flow velocity occure when air speeds through a gap, you only have to ask yourself why it is that draughts always close doors and never open them? Fig 23 will help to explain. It doesn't matter which way the air is flowing, when it rushes through the gap between the door and the door frame, the pressure on that side of the door will drop and the door will slam shut.

Pressure remains the same

Airflow speeds through gap

Drop in pressure
Door slams shut

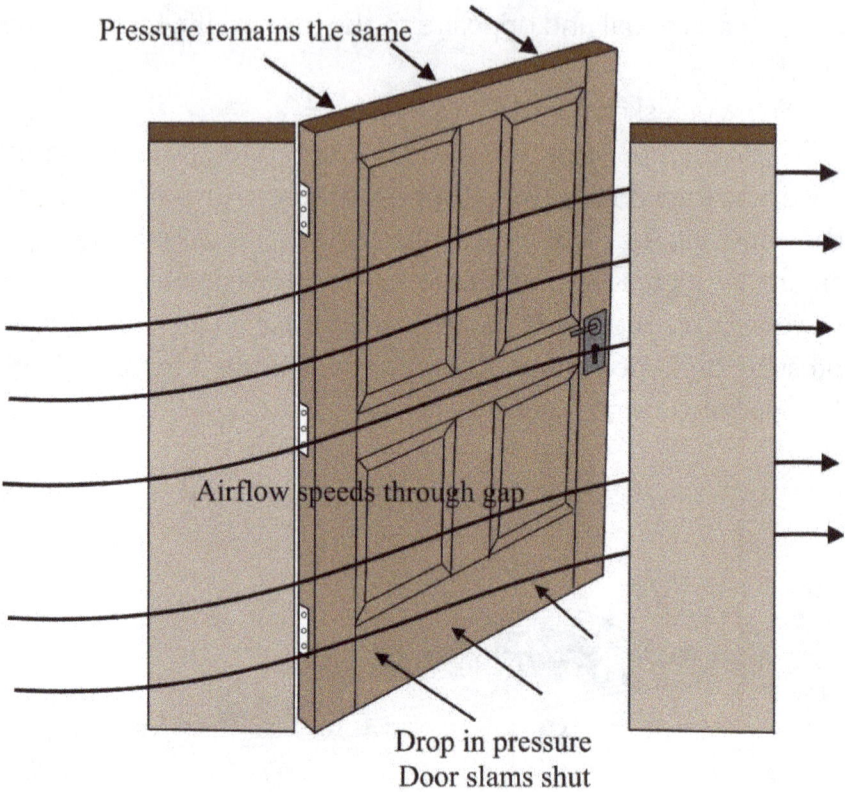

Fig 23 Pressure drops between door and frame so the greater pressure on the far side pushes the door shut.

Stalling

We know how to measure the wing's angle of attack, but how do we know which angle is the best? Well we know that lift increases if we increase the angle, but only up to a certain limit, after that it begins to fall off. Now although the actual amount of lift given by the wing when this fall off point is reached, varies a great deal according to the shape of the wing section, it is interesting to note that most wings, whatever their shape of section and whatever the air speed, seem to reach this drop off point, at about the same angle, and that's between 15° and 20°.

The reason for the fall off in lift at this kind of angle is because, at this angle, the airflow over the top of the wing changes from being a nice smooth flow, to one that is broken up into eddies and turbulence, destroying the smooth downwash and consequently the lift, Fig 24. This phenomenon is called stalling and it is probably one of the most studied aspects of flight.

This phenomenon of stalling or the breakup of streamlined airflow, is not unique to wing sections however, as we know from experiments done in wind tunnels with venturi tubes.

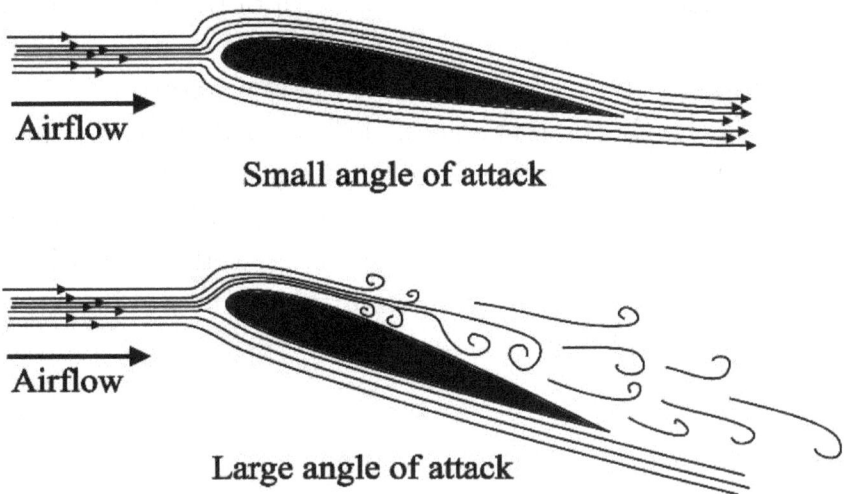

Small angle of attack

Large angle of attack

Fig 24 Air flow breaks down when the angle of attack reaches a certain point

So far, we have mainly have looked at the airflow through a venturi tube and over the surface of a wing in terms of how the airflow affects the pressure but now we are going it look at how the change of pressure effects the airflow.

Any fluid will flow easily from an area of high pressure to an area of low pressure, there is what is known as a "favourable pressure gradient," in effect, the air is flowing downhill as far as pressure is concerned. This is what is happening between the entrance to a venturi tube and the throat, or over the top surface of our wing up to the point of maximum camber. However, after the throat in a venturi tube or the point of maximum camber on our wing, the pressure is increasing, the pressure gradient becomes adverse, and it is as if the air is flowing uphill. If we're not careful....it could stall!

We have seen that if we increase the angle of attack to a certain point, between 15° and 20° the smooth airflow breaks up into eddies and lift is lost. Well the same thing happens in a venturi tube if we make the throat too narrow or expand the tube too suddenly after the throat. Although the front part of the wing section and the entry and throat of the venturi tube, seem to experience nearly all of the effect so far as reduction of pressure is concerned, they are entirely dependent for this effect on the shape and angle of the rear portion of the wing and the expanding exit portion of the venturi tube.

The airflow over the wing is extremely sensitive to both the exact shaping of the whole wing section and the angle of attack, get either of them wrong and the airflow will break up and the wing will stall.

More about Lift and Drag

Now I have a bit of a confession to make, I misled you a little bit about lift and drag but I did it because I didn't want to confuse the issue too early on. I told you that there was a force acting on the wing in two direction, up and back, and that the "up" part of the force was lift and the "back" part was drag. I now have to qualify that statement and say that it is only true when our aircraft is travelling horizontal to the ground, that is, in straight and level flight.

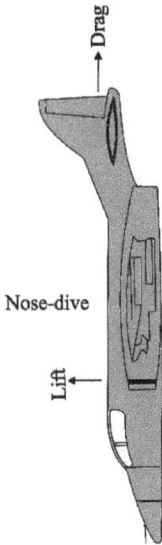

The real definition of lift is, that part of the force acting on a wing which is at right angles to the direction of travel, or the direction of the airflow, which amounts to the same thing. The real definition of drag is, that part of the force acting on a wing that is parallel to the airflow. So, you can see that the upwards and backwards ideas of lift and drag are only correct in horizontal flight, if the aircraft is in a nose-dive, the lift would be horizontal and the drag would be vertical, as in Fig 25.

Fig 25

Drag and speed

Both lift and drag are increased with speed but If you ask people how much they think drag is increased with an increase in speed, most people will guess that at double the speed, you will experience twice the amount of drag, but the truth is actually very different. At double the speed, lift and drag are around four times as much and for three times the speed they are nine times as much and for ten times the speed they are multiplied by one hundred, Fig 26. Lift and drag are proportional to the square of the speed.

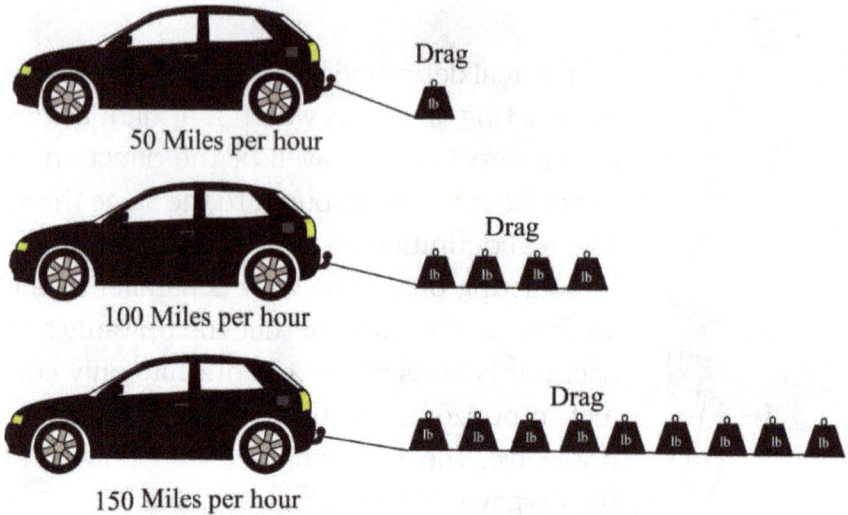

Fig 26. Lift and drag are proportional to the square of the speed

Lift and drag are also dependent on the size of the body, large bodies having more drag than small bodies of the same shape. At one time it was just regarded as being dependent on the frontal shape or its cross-sectional area when viewed from the front, the greater the frontal area the greater the drag.

Now however, because aircraft have become much more streamlined in shape, we think much more in terms of a body's overall surface area as skin friction has become of much more relative importance compared to form drag. It is now more cor-rect to say that resistance, or drag, is proportional to surface area, after all, provided bodies are of a similar shape it matters little whether we compare frontal areas or overall surface areas, a two inch cube will have four times the frontal area of a one inch cube and it will also have four times the surface area, and therefore, by both laws, four times the resistance, (at the same speed.) Fig 27.

Frontal area 1" x 1" = 1 sq inch
Surface area 1 sq inch x 6 = 6 sq inch

Frontal area 2" x 2" = 4 sq inch
Surface area 4 sq inch x 6 = 24 sq inch

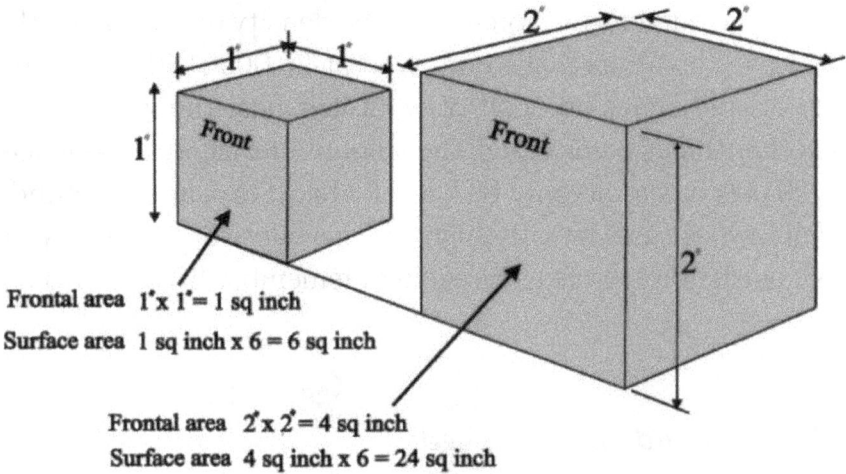

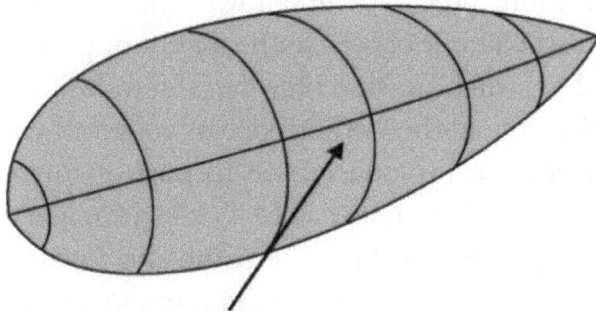

More streamlined shape means a reduction in form drag but an increase in skin friction

Fig 27. A two-inch cube will have four times the frontal area of a one-inch cube and it will also have four times the overall surface area

If however, our cube is reformed to have a more streamline body shape, the form drag will be very much reduced because of the better shape but we must not forget that there will be an increase in skin friction owing to the larger surface area and the greater velocity of airflow over it. What this means in practice is that, although it may not be worth polishing our cube, it would be worth polishing the more streamlined shape. In the case of lift it is usual to consider the Plan area of the wing. The other thing that influences the amount of lift and drag is the density of the air, the denser the air the greater the forces it produces, but let's not forget that the density of the air greatly decreases as we gain altitude, even at 20,000 ft. the air density is only about one half of what it is near the ground. So, all other things being equal, the amount of drag we experience at 20,000 ft. should only be half of what it is near the ground. Well in that case, let's fly high and have less drag, I hear you say, but before you get too excited, remember lift will also be reduced.

Air speed and ground speed

We performed the experiment with the stiff cardboard indoors and in still air but of course the air out of doors is very seldom still, there will be a wind blowing, and we will very soon notice that if you hold the leading edge of your stiff cardboard facing the wind, you no longer have to push it forward to feel the lifting force. That is because it doesn't make any difference whether you are pushing the cardboard forward in still air, or whether the cardboard is held still in moving air, all that matters is that the cardboard and the air are moving in relation to each other.

The speed at which our cardboard or an aircraft moves through the air or the air moves over the cardboard is known as the, air-speed. Now the air speed of an aircraft must not be confused with its ground-speed, because the speed of an aeroplane through the air is not the same as its speed over the ground. We are so used to talking about speed in relation to the ground that we tend to forget that aeroplanes fly in the air and have no contact with the ground unless landing or taking off. Not only is there a difference between air speed and ground speed, there is also a difference between the direction of travel of an aeroplane through the air compared to the direction it travels over the ground.

We are going to look at the difference between air speed and ground speed in a little more depth. When flying from A to B it will make a difference to the time taken whether the wind is with us or against us, and the difference in time will be greater the larger the distance between A and B. The ground speed will matter a great deal when calculating the journey time, but the air speed and therefore the lift and drag will be the same in both cases. An aeroplane in flight is always traveling against a headwind. When observing an aircraft from the ground we may say there is a headwind or a tailwind or even a sidewind but to those on the aircraft itself there is only a headwind.

Now ask yourselves the following questions:

Question A: If the normal airspeed of an aircraft is 80 mph and it is traveling west to east with a following 100 mph gale, in what direction would a flag on the aircraft be flying?

Question B: In what direction will the flag fly if the gale is from the north but the aircraft is still heading east?

Question C: In what direction would the flag fly in a free balloon that is traveling with a steady 30 mph wind from the north?

Question D: An aeroplane has enough fuel to fly for four hours at 100 mph. If there is no wind, how far can it fly from its base and get home again?

Question E: Will the aeroplane of question D have the same range of action if there is a steady 20 mph wind?

Question F: If you are asked to handicap aeroplanes of different speeds in a race in which they are required to fly from A to B and back again, will the speed of the wind at the time make any difference to your handicapping?

Answers: A = Directly backwards. B = Directly backwards. C = Downwards, the flag would not fly. D = 200 miles. E = No. F = Yes.

If you have answered all six question correctly, then I salute you, if however, you struggled with E and F, thinking that what you would lose when the wind was against you, you would gain when it was with you, I will explain further.

The answer to E is no because, to have the same range the aeroplane would still have to complete two, two hundred-mile legs, one with the twenty mph wind and one against. Assuming it is the outward leg that is against the wind, (it doesn't actually matter which leg is with or against,) this would give the plane a ground speed of 80 mph, meaning that it would take two and a half hours to cover the two hundred miles out. This would mean that the aeroplane could fly for a further one and a half hours at a ground speed of 120 mph, covering one hundred and eighty miles. Our unfortunate pilot would have to land twenty miles short of his base. If your route is not directly with or against the wind, the calculation is more difficult, but whichever direction you fly your range will be less than 200 miles.

As for question F, let's say that the distance between A and B is 60 miles and the wind-speed is 60 mph as shown below. Start your slower machine, let's say with an air-speed of 60mph first and it will have a ground speed of 120 mph on the outward leg, reaching B in half an hour. Then it will turn around to start back, but unfortunately it will not be going anywhere! Although it will have an airspeed of sixty miles per hour, its groundspeed will be zero. It doesn't matter how much later you start your faster plane, it will always win, Fig 28.

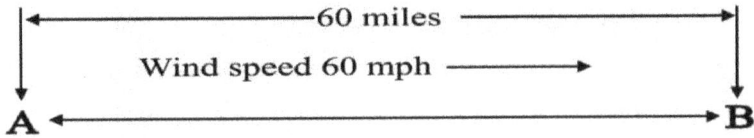

|←————————————60 miles ————————————→|

Wind speed 60 mph ——————→

A ←————————————————————————————→ B

Aeroplane with
air speed 60 mph

Ground speed on outward journey = 120 mph
Ground speed on return journey   =   nil mph

Aeroplane with
air speed 120 mph

Ground speed on outward journey = 180 mph
Ground speed on return journey   =   60 mph

Fig 28

Direction relative to the air or ground

We now know that we have to be careful to distinguish between air-speed and ground-speed, but we must also distinguish between the direction an aeroplane is traveling, relative to the air or relative to the ground.

In question B we had an aeroplane traveling from west to east with a wind blowing from the north, so although the aeroplane will be pointing east it will in fact travel crabwise over the ground in a south easterly direction, Fig 29.

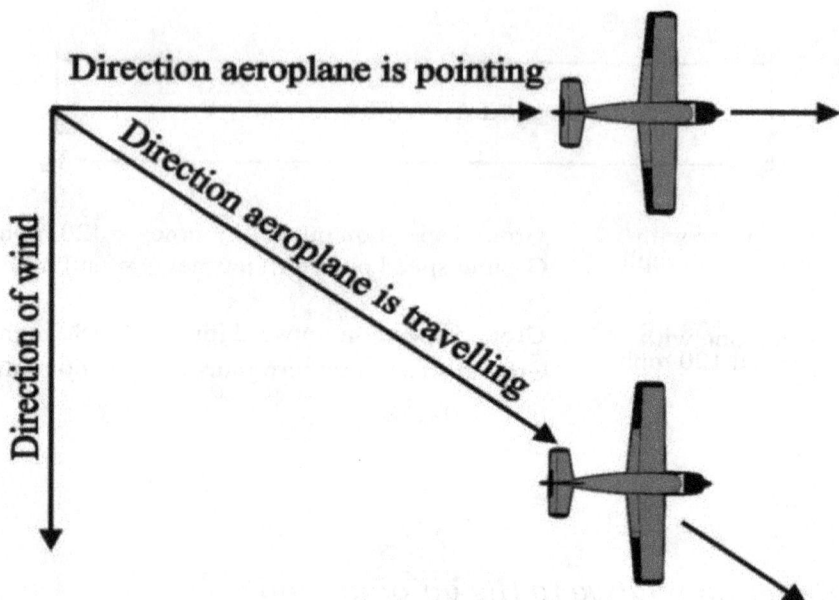

Fig 29

There is another, maybe less obvious aspect, to this business of the direction relative to the air or relative to the ground. An aeroplane that climbs or descends against a head wind will appear to climb or descend more steeply when viewed from the ground, although its path of climb relative to the air will be the same as in calm air or a following wind, Fig 30.

The difference between air direction and ground direction is even more marked when the wind itself is ascending, as in a thermal or blowing up the slope of a hill. Anyone who has ever been gliding will know that a glider or sailplane can be seen from the ground as climbing and maybe even flying backwards, whereas relative to the air it is always gliding downwards and forwards.

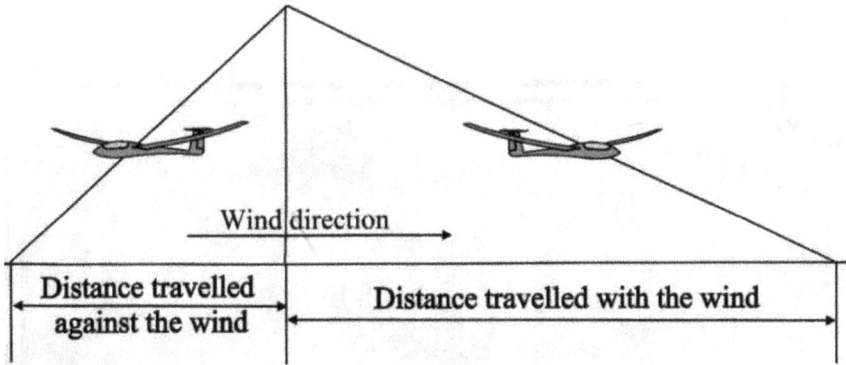

Fig 30. Effect of wind on angle of descent relative to the ground

More lift and Drag

Darren Harbar Photography

Chapter 4

More Lift and Drag

So, lift is our friend, it's what we require in order to fly, but we can't have it without drag, and drag is our enemy, it's always trying to prevent us moving forward through the air, which is what we need to do to get airflow over the wings and obtain lift. Can we increase lift without increasing drag? The answer is, sometimes.

If we increase lift by increasing speed or increasing wing area or even flying in denser air, then we will increase drag in the same proportion, double the lift, double the drag. However, if we increase lift by increasing the wing camber or by increasing the angle of attack, then we will still get an increase in drag, but not necessarily to the same extent. Now there are times when we want lift even at the expense of increasing drag, this is certainly true when we want a low landing speed, but remember that we can only increase the angle of attack up to about 20°. As for altering the wing camber, well certain wing sections will suite one type of aeroplane and other sections will suite another. A wing section that is good for a heavy cargo plane or a bomber will not be as suitable for a plane that needs high speeds, like a fighter.

Up until now we have only talked about drag as if it is just one entity, but in actual fact there are different kinds of drag, and we will look at those now.

If you pull an object of any shape or form through the air you will experience resistance or drag, it's a fact of nature that we have to accept, the only thing you can do is try to minimise it. If you're driving a van and you have an advertising sign strapped to your roof you will have a large amount of drag created by it. Now, maybe you consider the increase in the amount of petrol you will use to be worth it in order to get your companies name known, but you could save drag and therefore money by removing the sign, your van doesn't need it to function as a van. The same is true for aircraft, if you can do away with something that is causing drag but is not needed to be able to fly, then that's a sensible thing to do, but of course there are some things that are essential to have, the wings for example, they cause drag but we need them to supply lift. For that reason, some people refer to the drag caused by things that we need to supply lift as "Active Drag or Wing Drag." Now this wing drag is itself made up of different kinds of drag.

Induced Drag

Where the air flows around the wing tip, it tends to flow from the region of high pressure below the wing to the area of low pressure above. This causes the airflow over the top of the wing to flow slightly inward and the airflow over the bottom to flow slightly outwards, thus, when the two meet at the trailing edge they cross over each other forming little vortices. These vortices migrate towards the wing tip where they form one larger vortex. The resulting vortices change the speed and direction of the airflow behind the trailing edge, deflecting it downwards, that outside the span is deflected upwards. Thus, the net direction of the air which actually passes the aerofoil is in a downward direction, and so the lift, which is at right angles to the air flow is slightly backwards and thus contributes to the drag, Fig 31. The drag formed in this way is called induced drag because it is a result of the downward velocity "induced" by the wing tip vortices.

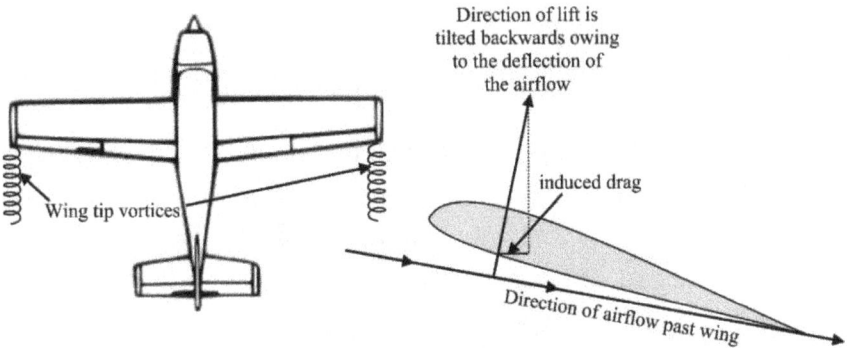

Fig 31. Induced drag caused by wing tip vortices

Parasite Drag

An aeroplane is more than just a wing that produces lift, it has a fuselage, a tail plane, engines, fuel tanks and a lot more. These things, although they may be necessary, may not contribute towards the lift, but they all produce drag and that drag is therefore referred to as, "parasite drag."

Now there are two things that can be done to reduce parasite drag, one obviously, is to do away with the component that is producing it altogether and the design of a sleek modern air-craft is now a far cry from the early days of struts and wires and fixed undercarriage. The other thing that can be done is to design the component as aerodynamically as possible so as to reduce the drag it produces to a minimum and that's what we'll look at next.

Form Drag

That drag which is produced by the shape or form of a body is called, form drag. We saw when we looked at the effects of size on drag in Fig 27, how streamlining can be used to reduce the amount of drag a body creates. Streamlining basically means designing a shape so that airflow, or water, passes over it in smooth streamlines without causing eddies and we now know that this can reduce drag by significant amounts and that all modern vehicles, not just aircraft, now have streamlining in their design, Fig 32.

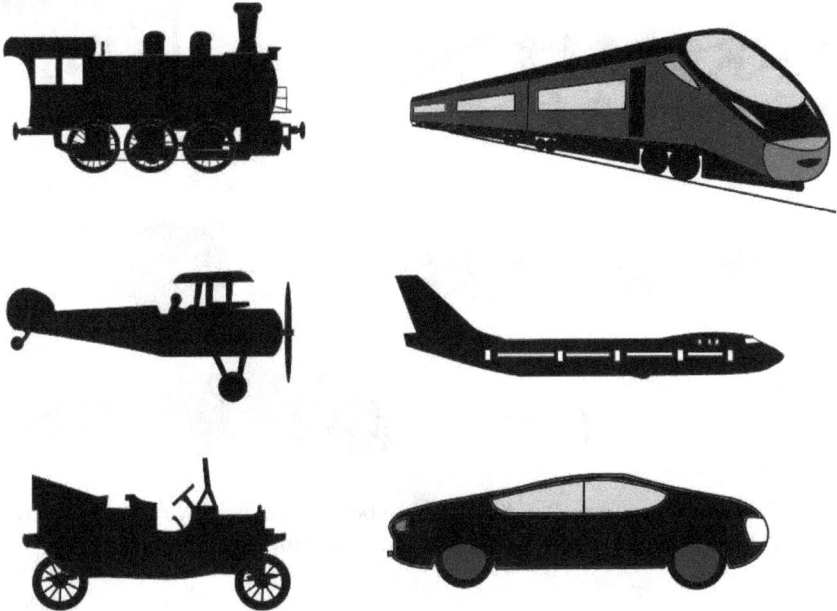

Fig 32. Modern vehicles now have streamlined shapes

For some reason it appears that, although designers realised early on that it was better to design the hulls of boats to "cut" through the water to reduce resistance, the same importance was not given to air resistance until later, possibly because water could be seen and felt more easily than air and the resistance was more obvious and pronounced. There was a time when the pilots of early bi-planes laughed at the idea of using streamlined or "RAF" cable instead of the standard round type, believing that the amount of drag saved would be so small, it wasn't worth the effort. Even now people are amazed at just how much difference streamlining can make. If you look at Fig 33, the drag on the large flat plate at the top can be reduced by as much as 95 percent by the streamlining illustrated at the bottom.

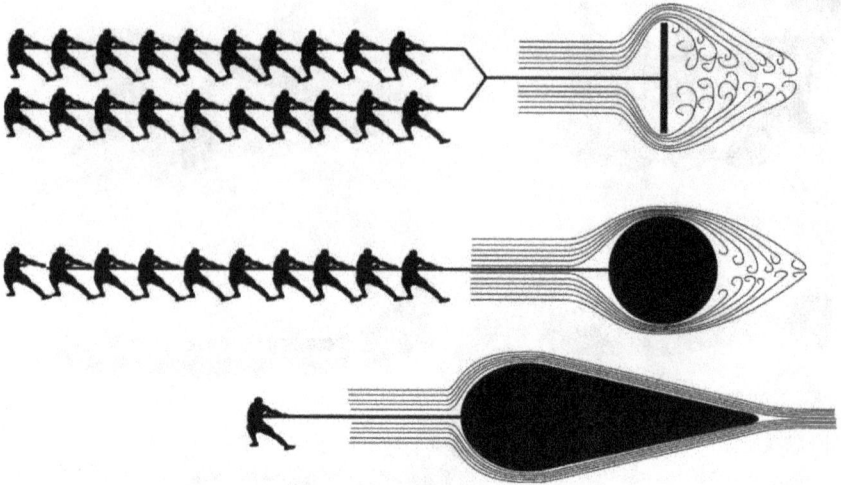

Fig 33. How the drag on a flat disc (top) can be reduced, first by rounding into a ball (middle) and then by as much as 95% with full streamlining (bottom)

Skin Friction

The comparative roughness of the skin of an object will also affect the amount of drag it produces, a rough surface, un-surprisingly, producing more drag than a smooth one. Now speed is an important factor when considering skin friction be-cause the benefits of a smooth surface are greater at higher speeds. A smooth surface also compliments the streamlining of a body, the overall difference in the amount of drag between a smooth or a rough surface on a badly shaped body may not be great, but the difference between the two on a streamlined body most certainly is.

The Boundary Layer

We have talked about the airflow over the wing and how the flow over the top speeds up compared to the flow under the wing, but we have regarded this airflow as a single entity, "the airflow," but in fact there are two elements to it.

The closest layer to the surface of a body is the boundary layer and this actually stays virtually motionless relative to the bodies surface, the next layer then moves over this stationary layer at a small velocity and the next at a slightly higher velocity and so on until it reaches the full velocity of the general airflow. If you find this difficult to accept, next time you find a layer of dust on the bonnet of your car on a dry day, take it for a fast drive and observe how any leaves blow off straight away but the dust remains. Even if you go very fast, (don't break any speed limit!) the dust will remain because it is in the thin layer of air that moves with the car, the boundary layer.

The details of the flow within the boundary layer are very important for many problems in aerodynamics, including wing stall, skin friction drag, and the heat transfer that occurs in high speed flight. Unfortunately, the physical and mathematical details of boundary layer theory are way beyond the scope of this book and are topics usually studied at late undergraduate or graduate level.

Viscosity

The viscosity or stickiness of a fluid is the tendency for one layer of the fluid to stick to the next layer. It is easy to think in terms of fluids like treacle as being sticky or viscose but we don't very often think of air as being sticky and that's because the viscosity of air is only really effective in the small boundary layer, outside of the boundary layer the air behaves as if it were non viscose.

We now know that the airflow over a wing that is inclined at a small angle will look like that in Fig 34. Notice that the air flows faster over the top than beneath and that there is an upwash in front of the wing and a downwash behind.

Now, what I am about to say next is a little difficult to imagine for some but helpful to try. Imagine that you are somehow floating along beside the wing and with the airflow. You would see the air in front of the wing was moving up relative to you, the airflow over the top would be moving towards the back of the wing, the airflow at the back would be moving down, and importantly, the air under the wing, because it would be moving slower than the air on top, would *appear* to be moving backwards. Relative to you it would almost look as if the air was circulating around the wing.

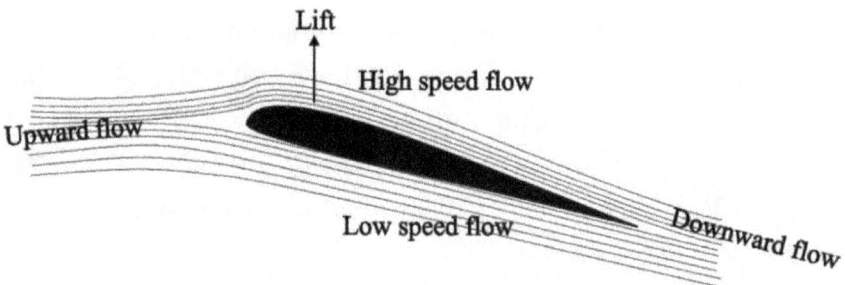

Fig 34

Remember, this is how it would *appear* to you, *do not think that any particles of air actually travel around the wing,* it is all about the motion relative to you.

It may be easier to visualise this *apparent* circulation of air if, instead of a wing moving through the air, we think of a rotating cylinder. The boundary layer will rotate with the cylinder and if you study Fig 35 you will see that this creates an upwash in front, a downwash behind, an increase in speed over the top and a decrease below, just like our wing. This also means that there will be a decrease in pressure above and an increase below, creating lift.

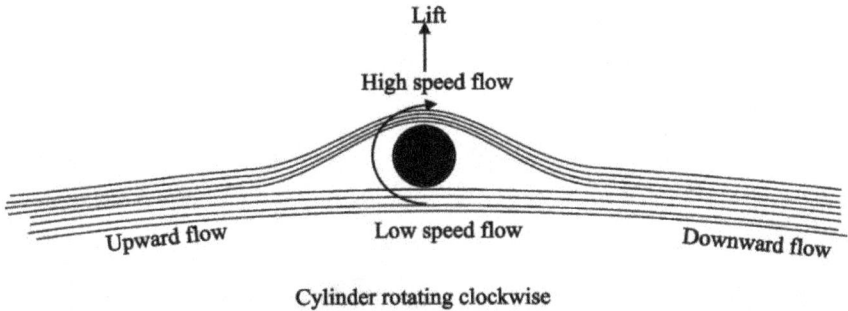

Cylinder rotating clockwise

Fig 35. A rotating cylinder can produce lift

If you still need convincing, just think what happens when a tennis player puts "top" or "bottom" on a ball or a golfer inadvertently imparts sidespin to his ball, you will know that the ball is caused to swerve as it travels through the air. It is "lift" that causes the swerve, remember that lift does not have to be up, it is that part of the force acting on a wing which is at right angles to the direction of travel, or the direction of the airflow, which amounts to the same thing, so it can be up, sideways or even down, Fig 36 and Fig 25.

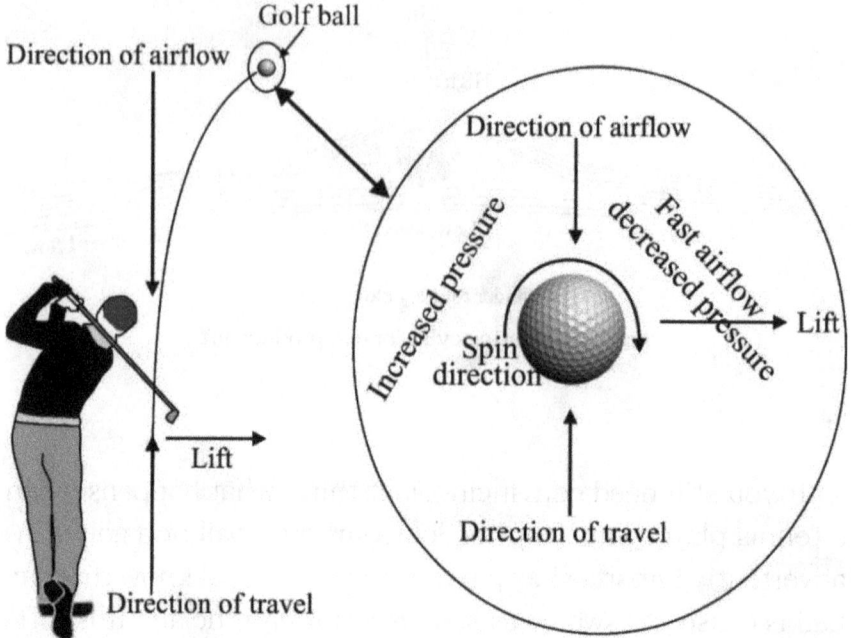

Fig 36. Spin imparted to a ball will decrease airflow over one side and increase it the other, creating lift and pulling the ball off line

The perfect aerofoil

So, after all we have learnt so far, what is the shape of the perfect aerofoil or wing. Well it would be one with no drag at all, but we know that is impossible, we also know that different shapes suit different kinds of aircraft and we know that a different shape is required for slow landing speeds, so on a perfect wing we would be able to alter the size and shape of it without adding anything to its weight and I'm not sure if that will ever be possible, but there are some things we can do.

Flaps.

Nowadays, flaps are fitted to almost all aeroplanes and are designed to increase the camber of the wing for extra lift when required, such as when landing or to a lesser extent, taking off, they are normally mounted on the trailing edge and are retracted during normal cruising flight. When deployed, flaps not only increase lift they also increase drag, slowing the aircraft down for approach and landing, they also reduce the stalling speed so that an aeroplane can fly safely at a lower airspeed. An unintended, though useful side effect of the flaps is that on many aircraft they decrease the pitch angle, lowering the nose and giving the pilots a better view of the runway.

There are many different designs of flaps used, with the specific choice depending on the size, speed and complexity of the aircraft on which they are to be used, as well as the era in which the aircraft was designed. Plain flaps, slotted flaps and Fowler flaps are the most common. Krueger flaps are positioned on the leading edge of the wings and are used on many jet airliners, Fig 37.

The Fowler, Fairey-Youngman and Gouge types of flap increase the wing area in addition to changing the camber. The larger lifting surface reduces wing loading, hence further reducing the stalling speed.

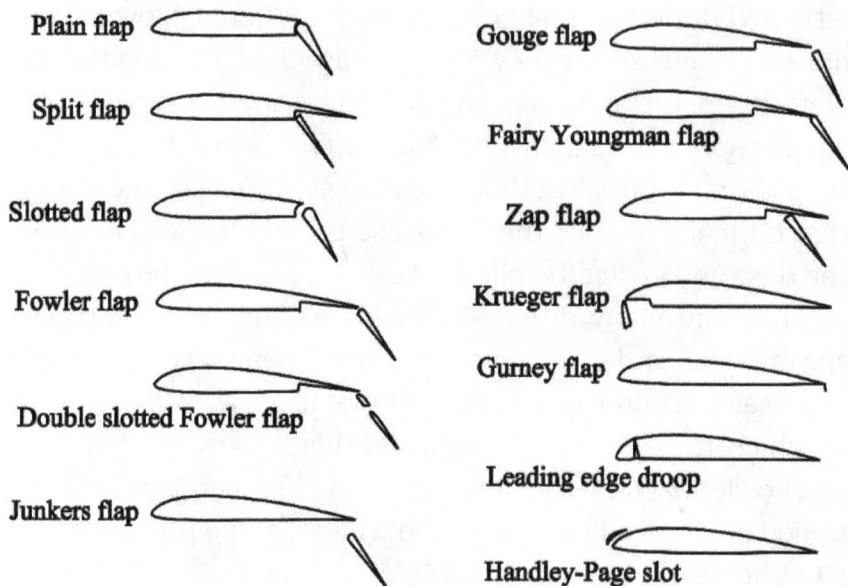

Fig 37

It was mentioned earlier that stalling is caused by the airflow over the wing breaking away from the top surface and forming eddies. Slots are designed to postpone this from happening by allowing the air to pass through a gradually narrowing gap near the leading edge, so that it picks up speed just like going through a venturi tube and is kept close to the wing surface. The gap through which the air passes is the slot and the small aerofoil which forms the top surface is called a slat, see Fig 37 Handley-Page slot.

Aspect Ratio

As well as considering the section of a wing we also have to look at its aspect ratio. The aspect ratio of a wing is the ratio of its "span" or length to its "chord" or breadth, thus a long narrow wing like that of a glider, will have a high aspect ratio, whereas a short wide wing, like that of a biplane, will have a low ratio. It is of course possible to have wings with the same surface area but very different aspect ratios. We know that we cannot completely eliminate induced drag but it can be reduced and this is where aspect ratio comes in. We know from experiments that there is a small but quite definite increase in efficiency as we increase the aspect ratio, keeping the area the same, Fig 38.

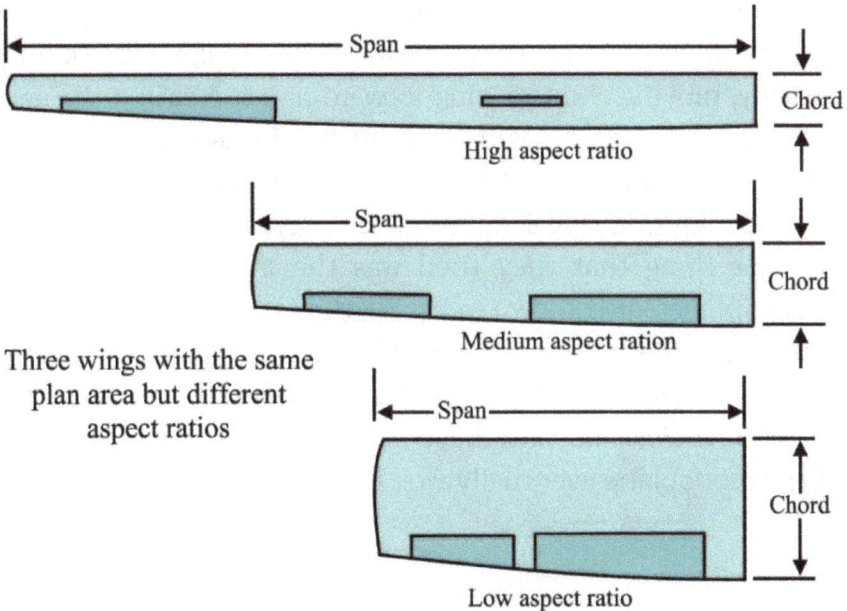

Span

Chord

High aspect ratio

Span

Chord

Medium aspect ration

Three wings with the same plan area but different aspect ratios

Span

Chord

Low aspect ratio

Fig 38

Biplanes

We know that large wing areas are good for producing lift and therefore it stands to reason that supplying an aeroplane with two wings would give us double the amount of lift without having to have an enormously long wingspan. Two short wings also mean that the aircraft is easier to manoeuvre on the ground and structurally more sound. So why are we not designing biplanes anymore? Well, the simple answer is that there is interference between the two wings which reduces the efficiency of both.

At first, designers tried increasing the gap between the wings, but it was found that very large gaps were needed to make a worthwhile difference and this added weight and structural problems. Next, they staggered the wings, Fig 39, and actually, moving the top wing forward and increasing the gap between it and the bottom one a little did lesson the interference, it also gave the pilot better visibility and easier access to the cockpit, so this adaptation was soon generally adopted. Another thing that they tried was the introduction of the "Sesquiplane," also shown in Fig 39, the sesquiplane was still a biplane but the lower wing was only half the area of the upper one and this reduced the amount of interference considerably, but nevertheless, despite these improvements the advantages of the monoplane eventually won out.

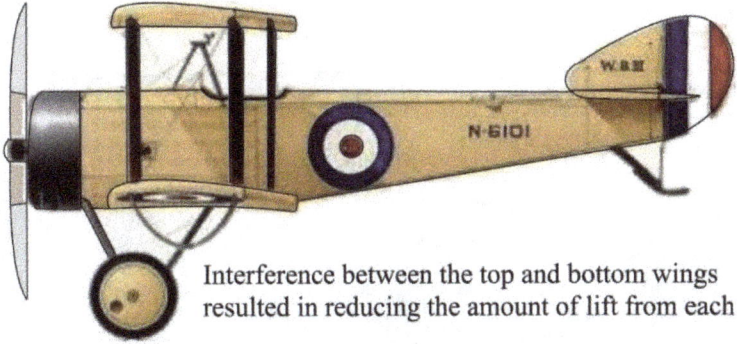

Interference between the top and bottom wings resulted in reducing the amount of lift from each

Staggered top and bottom wings reduces the amount of interference and supplies more lift

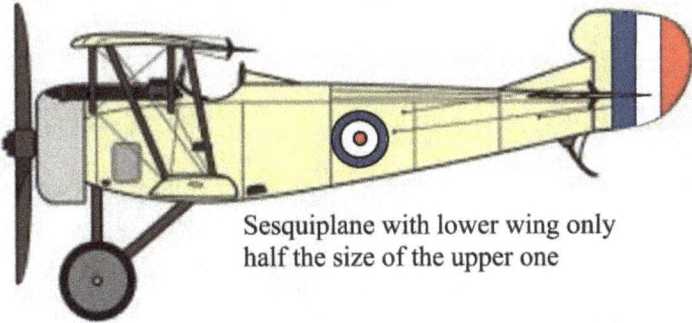

Sesquiplane with lower wing only half the size of the upper one

Fig 39

Actual Flight

Darren Harbar Photography

Chapter 5

Actual Flight

Albert Einstein published his theory of relativity in two parts, "the special theory," concerning objects traveling in a straight line at a constant velocity and the "general theory," concerning all other objects, ones that are accelerating, that is, altering speed or direction. Likewise, we can divide flight into two categories, straight and level flight and steering or manoeuvring flight.

Straight and Level Flight.

Now generally, pilots do not spend a great deal of time flying straight and level, with the possible exception of long-haul flights, but it is the place we must start. An aeroplane in flight has four forces acting on it, we have already looked at two of them, lift and drag, but the other two are no less important and they are "thrust" the force that keeps the aeroplane moving forwards so that there is airflow over the wings and the force of "gravity" that gives the aeroplane weight and which the lift has to overcome, Fig 40.

These forces must be balanced for the aircraft to maintain steady flight, now that's simple to understand as far as lift and weight are concerned, it's easy to see that the amount of lift has to be equal to the overall weight of the plane for it to fly, but the amount of thrust must also be equal to the amount of drag.

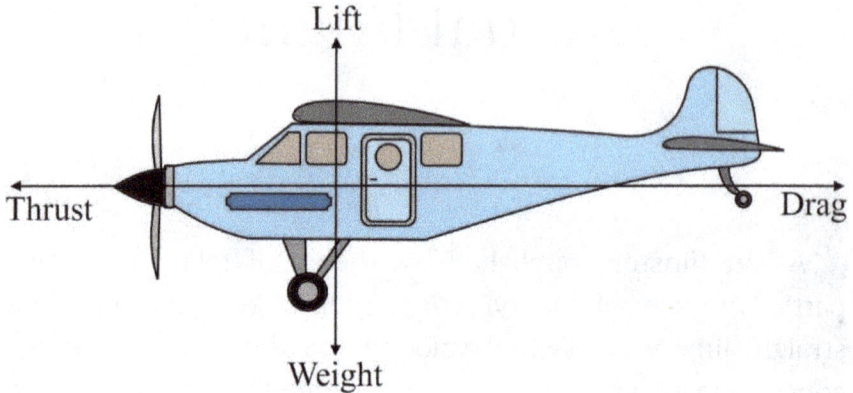

Fig 40. The four forces acting on an aeroplane in flight

A look at Thrust

Every action has an equal and opposite reaction, we've heard that before but what does it mean in practice? In a rowing boat, you dip the oars into the water and pull, this action pushes water away towards the back of the boat and so the oar, and consequently the boat, is propelled forwards with equal force. If you stand on a skateboard and throw a cricket ball away from you, you'll begin to move in the opposite direction, and if you keep throwing cricket balls you will keep moving, throw with more force and you'll move quicker. The problem is, of course, that you very soon run out of cricket balls. The rowing boat on the other hand is surrounded by water and as long as we keep pushing the water back with our oar the boat will keep moving forward. Our aeroplane is surrounded by air, and although air is not as good a medium as water for pushing against, it still works in the same way, using the same principle, and it's a lot easier and more effective than carrying hundreds of cricket balls. All we need is some method of pushing the air backwards.

The first method adopted was the propeller, a rather simple but nevertheless effective way of pushing the air backwards and so propelling the aircraft forwards. The rotating propeller blades produce a backward force, or slipstream, of about the same diameter as the propeller itself. The propeller had its limitations however and it didn't take long for the jet engine to take over once it had been invented. There are two possible configurations for a propeller engine. If the propeller is mounted in front of the engine so that it pulls the engine for-ward, it is known a "tractor configuration". If on the other hand the propeller is mounted behind the engine, so that it pushes the engine forward it is known, unsurprisingly, as a "pusher configuration".

With a jet engine, air flows into the front of the engine where it is compressed, partly by the natural ram effect and partly by the engine itself, it's then heated with the aid of some fuel and then, having acquired extra energy, rushes out the back faster than it came in, Fig 41.

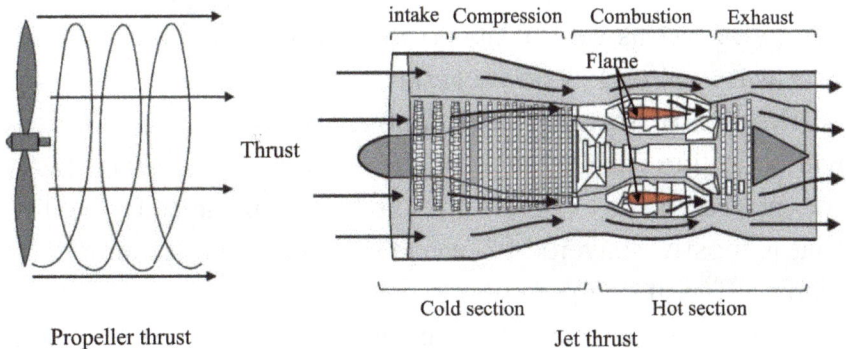

Fig 41. Propeller and jet thrust

There are different types of jet engine and even a turbo-prop where a turbine engine is used to drive propellers rather than suppling the thrust direct. We'll have another look at engines later in the book.

Balance

We have said that an aeroplane must have the four forces balanced to maintain straight and level flight but we must also consider their lines of force. If the centre of lift is far back from the centre of gravity the aeroplane will be nose-heavy, likewise if the line of thrust is high and the drag low. If the line of lift is forward of line of weight or thrust low and drag high then the aeroplane will be tail-heavy.

Now remember that the lift will be mainly supplied by the wings, so the position of those will determine the line of lift, but remember also that the centre of pressure is well forward of the centre of the wing and that it moves with changes to the angle of attack.

The line of weight will be through the centre of gravity, that is easy to establish on the finished aircraft, but not so easy during early design stages, and the designer also has to take into account the variable nature of the weight. The aeroplane has to be just as well balanced when full of fuel and passengers as it is when low on fuel and void of passengers.

The line of thrust is comparatively easy to establish as it will be in line with the axis of the engine. As for drag, this is the most difficult to determine the line of, because unlike lift, that is mostly delivered from one source, drag is generated by many different components.

Now. although it is necessary for thrust to equal drag and lift to equal weight, the two pairs of forces do not have to be equal, indeed, it is important that lift and weight are far greater than thrust and drag. The whole purpose of an aeroplane is to lift as much weight as possible with the minimum amount of thrust.

Why have a tailplane

If you look back at Fig 40 you will see that the lines of all four forces pass though one point and that would indeed create an equilibrium if weight equalled lift and trust equalled drag and there would be no tendency for the aircraft to rotate.

I have no idea what difficulties would be faced in arranging for the lines of all four forces to all pass through one point, but I do know that it is not advisable, and the reason is that there are occasions, when it is beneficial to have an aeroplane that is slightly nose-heavy. If for example, a pilot should suddenly lose thrust for some reason, he will need the aeroplane to very quickly adopt a nose-down attitude in order to put the aeroplane into a natural glide angle. Tail heaviness, on the other hand would tend to cause the aeroplane to stall.

The best way to make an aeroplane nose-heavy when it loses thrust is to arrange for the line of lift to be behind the line of weight. It doesn't have to be by much, just a few inches on a full-size aeroplane will be enough. If we do this however, we must take steps to prevent nose heaviness during normal horizontal flight when we have thrust. This can be achieved by arranging for the line of thrust to be low and the line of drag high, Fig 42.

Now the arrangement shown in Fig 42 is the one commonly adopted where practical considerations allow it, but because the forces of thrust and drag are smaller than those of lift and weight they would have to be further apart to produce the same effect and that may be difficult or even impossible to achieve.

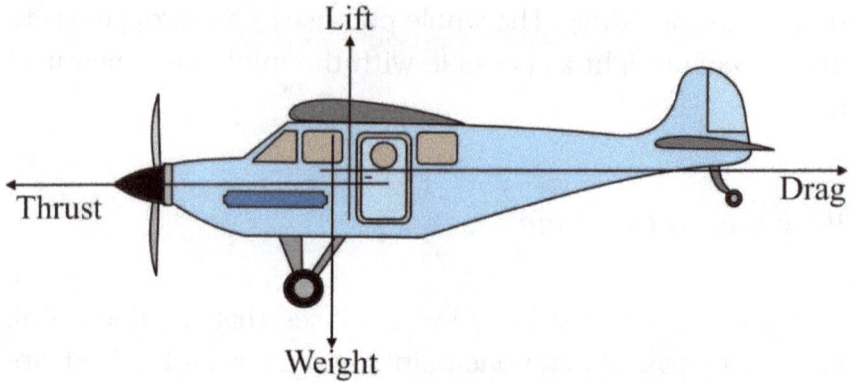

Fig 42. Line of drag is higher than line ofthrust and line of lift is behind the line of weight (centre of gravity)

If propellers are used, we are limited in lowering the line of thrust by the diameter of the propeller, which must of course clear the ground even when the aircraft is not in the air. With jet engines we have a little more room for manoeuvre but there are still limitations. What is needed is something that will counteract any out of balance tendencies if and when required and that much needed something is the *tail plane*.

Rolling Yawing and Pitching

So the purpose of the tail plane is to correct any out of balance effects of the four main forces, and at the rear of the horizontal tail plane are the elevators that are used to control the pitch of the aircraft, and at the rear of the vertical tail plane is the rudder, used to control yaw, the roll or banking of an aircraft is controlled by the ailerons that are located on the trailing edges of the wings near the wing tips, see Fig 43.

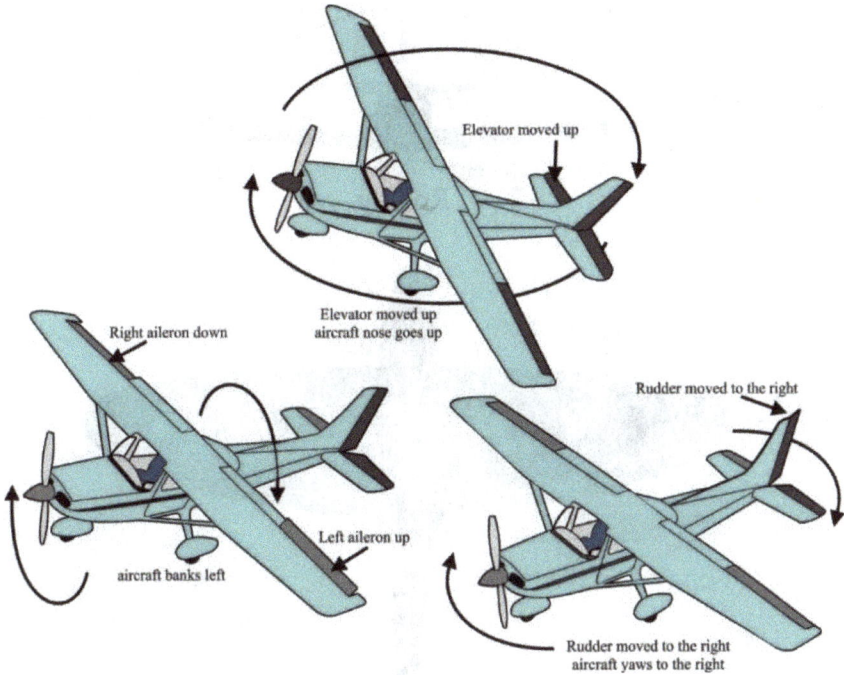

Elevator moved up

Elevator moved up
aircraft nose goes up

Right aileron down

Rudder moved to the right

Left aileron up

aircraft banks left

Rudder moved to the right
aircraft yaws to the right

Fig 43. The main control surfaces and their effects on attitude

The best way to think about how the control surfaces affect the attitude of the aircraft is to think of the aircraft as having three axis. The longitudinal axis, running from the front to the back through the centre of gravity; the lateral axis, running parallel with a line from wing tip to wing tip and also passing through the centre of gravity and the normal axis running up through the centre of gravity at right angles to the other two. The control surfaces cause the aircraft to rotate about these axes as shown in Figs 44.

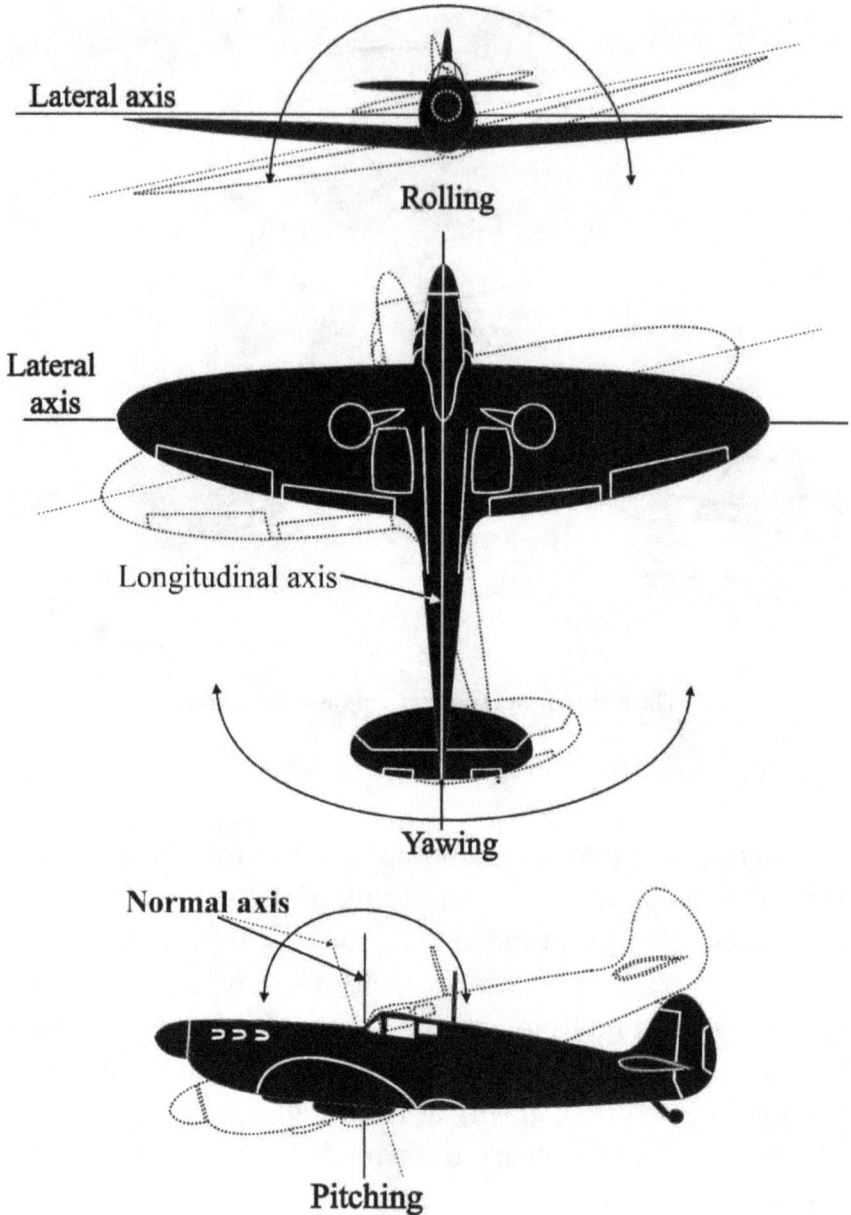

Fig 44. Rolling, yawing and pitching around the three axis

It's important to remember that these axes are fixed relative to the aircraft and move with it, so although the normal axis is vertical when the aircraft is in straight and level flight, it will no longer be so if the aircraft rolls or pitches see Fig 45.

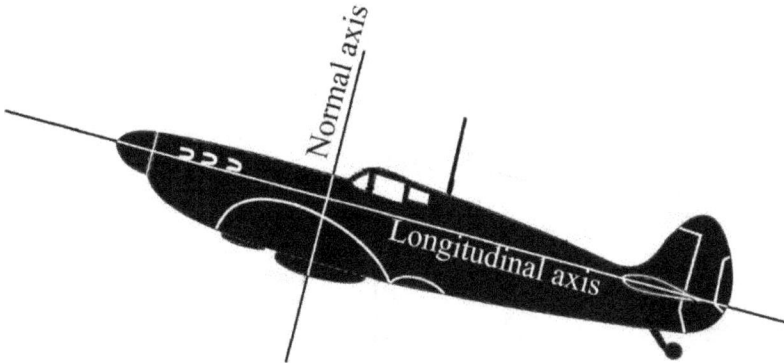

Fig 45. Normal and longitudal axes are relative to the aircraft and will no longer be vertical and horizontal if the aircraft rolls or pitches.

We'll look at each of the control surfaces in turn and start with the ailerons.

The Ailerons

The ailerons, which are located towards the tips of the wings on the trailing edge, see Fig 43, move up and down in opposition to one another, that is to say that if the right aileron is moved up the left will move down and visa versa. If an aileron is moved down this creates more force pushing the air under the wing down and this in turn creates more lift so the wing rises. On the other wing where the aileron moves up, there is less downward pressure under the wing and so a corresponding drop in the amount of lift generated, the combined effect causes the aircraft to bank or roll in the direction of least lift.

When the aircraft banks to one side the force of weight is no longer directly in line with the force of lift and this imbalance causes the aircraft to side-slip in the direction of bank, Fig 46.

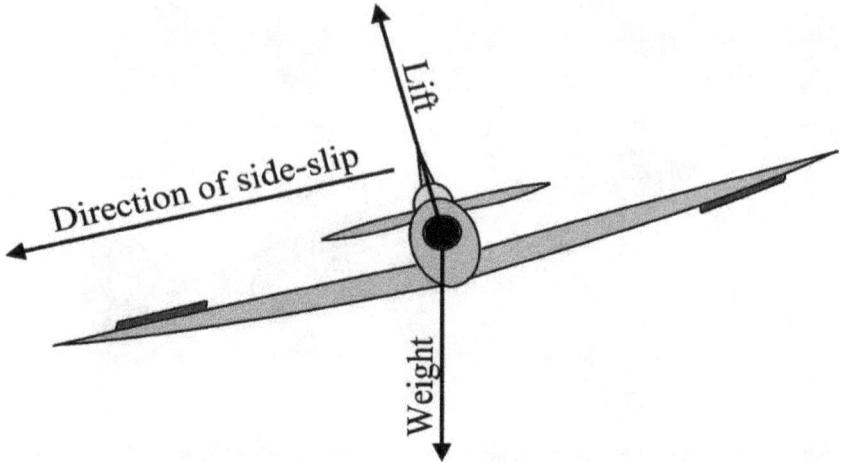

Fig 46. Aircraft will side-slip in the direction of bank

A secondary effect of the ailerons is to yaw the aircraft in the opposite direction to bank (adverse yaw), this is because the increase in lift in the up going wing also results in an increase in drag. This relatively small effect of adverse yaw is overcome by the pilot using a little rudder in the direction of bank. If rudder is not applied, the effect would soon be overcome anyway in most light aircraft, by a phenomenon called weathercocking. Because there is more fuselage and surface area behind the centre of gravity than there is in front of it, the force of the air rushing against the side of the aircraft as it side-slips will cause it to yaw in the direction of bank and the power of that rushing air soon overcomes the comparatively weak secondary effect of the ailerons. The net result is that when an aircraft banks right it will also *eventually* yaw to the right.

The Rudder

The rudder is situated vertically on the trailing edge of the tail-plane. When the rudder is moved to the right the air pushing against it will yaw the aircraft to the right about the normal axis. In light aircraft the pilot will use some rudder, that is controlled with the use of rudder pedals, when banking to initiate a nice smooth turn and avoid any adverse yaw. In gliders it is important to have a well-balanced turn, avoiding any slipping (not enough rudder) or skidding (too much rudder) in order not to lose unnecessary height.

When I was gliding, one of our instructors was in the habit of taking a plastic beaker of water with him that had a lid on it and in order to get us to make nice smooth turns, he would remove the lid of the beaker and hold it over our laps while getting us to initiate a steep turn. If we were successful in balancing the ailerons and the rudder the water would stay in the beaker throughout the turn, if not, we would return with an embarrassing wet patch in our lap. If you want to try a little experiment, fill a bucket about three quarters full with water, hold it by the handle and twirl around like a skater. The natural tendency is for your arms, including the one holding the bucket to lift away from your body and at the right speed you should be able to hold the bucket out horizontally without spilling any water, centrifugal force will keep it in the bucket.

So, a balanced turn is achieved by both banking and yawing the aircraft and I mentioned briefly that the rudder is controlled by the use of foot pedals. I can remember when I had my first lesson in a glider and we were told that pushing forward on the right pedal and pulling back on the left, moved the rudder to the right and therefore yawed the aircraft to the right, I accepted this as intuitive, but some of my fellow students didn't! They thought that to yaw the aircraft to the right, it was more intuitive to push forward the left pedal and back on the right, arguing that if you are riding a bike and want to turn right, that is what you do with the handlebars. Fig 47 shows how the rudder is controlled.

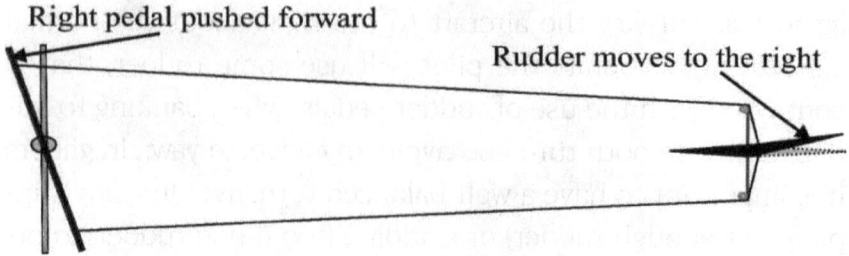

Right pedal pushed forward

Rudder moves to the right

Fig 47

Now I may have given slightly the wrong impression about the use of the rudder, as you may be thinking that the purpose of the rudder is to yaw the aircraft about the normal axis (sometimes called the yaw axis) but actually the opposite is true. The true main function of the rudder is to prevent yaw about the normal axis. In a nice balanced turn, the aircraft is not yawing about the normal axis at all, remember that the axes are always relative to the aircraft itself.

Let me attempt to explain further. If you want to turn right in an aeroplane you use the ailerons to bank the aircraft to the right, in effect, you increase the amount of lift generated by the left wing and decrease the amount of lift generated by the right wing, this in turn means an increase in drag on the left wing and a decrease in drag on the right wing. This will result in the aircraft yawing to the left, in the opposite direction to bank as explained. Now, since yaw is an undesirable thing that we want to eliminate, the pilot will apply a little right-hand rudder in order to eliminate the adverse left-hand yaw generated by the bank of the aircraft to the right, Fig 48.

Right hand rudder is applied
to counteract left hand yaw

Right aileron up

Left aileron down

Aircraft banks right but yaws to the left

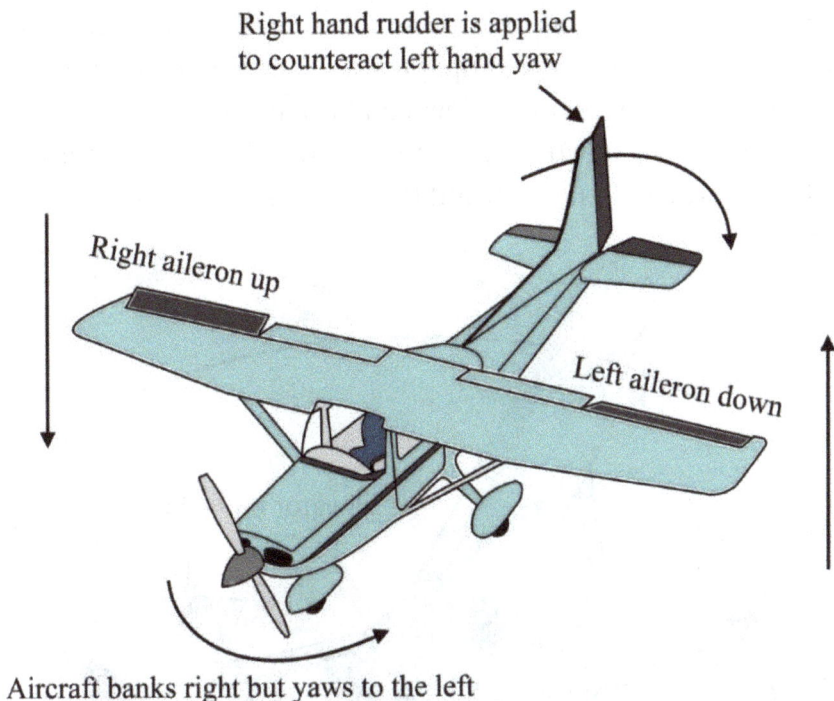

Fig 48. Rudder is used to eliminate adverse yaw

Now adverse yaw or aileron drag, is not a major problem
at high or cruising speeds and is easily overcome by applying
some rudder, however aileron drag can be a problem at low
speed and various methods have been tried to overcome it, including the use of slots, spoilers, frise ailerons and differential
ailerons.

The Elevators

The elevators are located on the trailing edge of the horizontal tail plane and can be operated by cables, levers or the
system may be power operated either hydraulically, pneumati-

cally or electrically, as indeed can any of the control surfaces. If the elevators are moved up, pressure is increased on the top of the tail plane forcing it down and the nose up, if the elevators are moved down air pressure against the bottom surface will push the tail plane up and the nose will drop, Fig 48A.

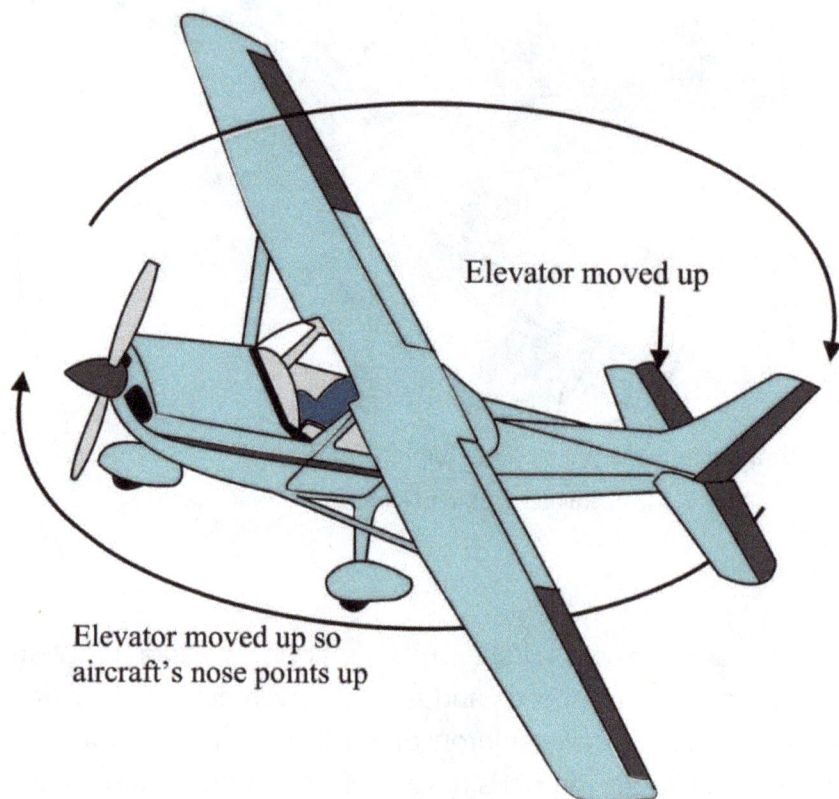

Elevator moved up

Elevator moved up so aircraft's nose points up

Fig 48A. The effect of the Elevators

Trim. Balancing the controls

On large aircraft the movement of the controls is power assisted, very much like the power steering on a car, but on many light aircraft some form of balance is required. The amount of pressure a pilot must exert to use the controls is not great but on a long journey, just keeping the controls central can be a strain.

One way to alleviate things is to have some small portion of the control surface in front of the hinge so that the airflow striking that portion helps the control surface to move in the required direction, see Fig 49. The examples shown here only show the control panels moved in one direction but obviously the effect is the same when moved in the opposite direction as well. Care must be taken when designing this system not to overdo the effect.

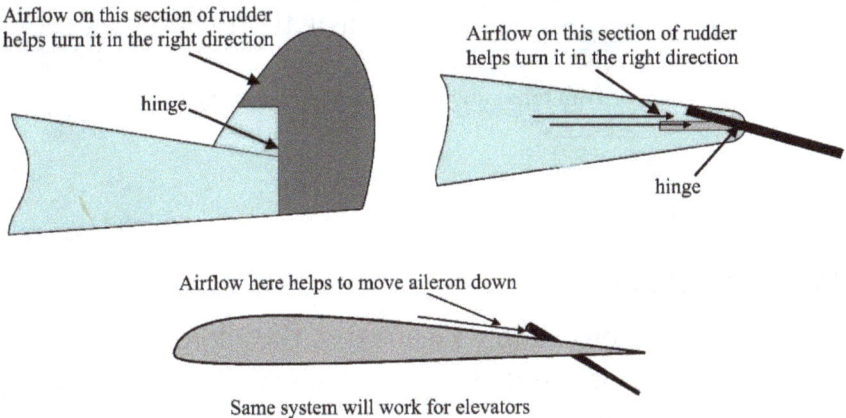

Airflow on this section of rudder helps turn it in the right direction

hinge

Airflow on this section of rudder helps turn it in the right direction

hinge

Airflow here helps to move aileron down

Same system will work for elevators

Fig 49. One way to balance control surfaces

Another way to ease the strain of holding control panels as required is the trim tab. This takes the form of a small control surface on the trailing edge of the main surface and when moved to one side, the air pressure on it moves the main control surface in the required direction, Fig 50.

Trim tab moved to the left
so rudder moves right.

Elevator trim tab

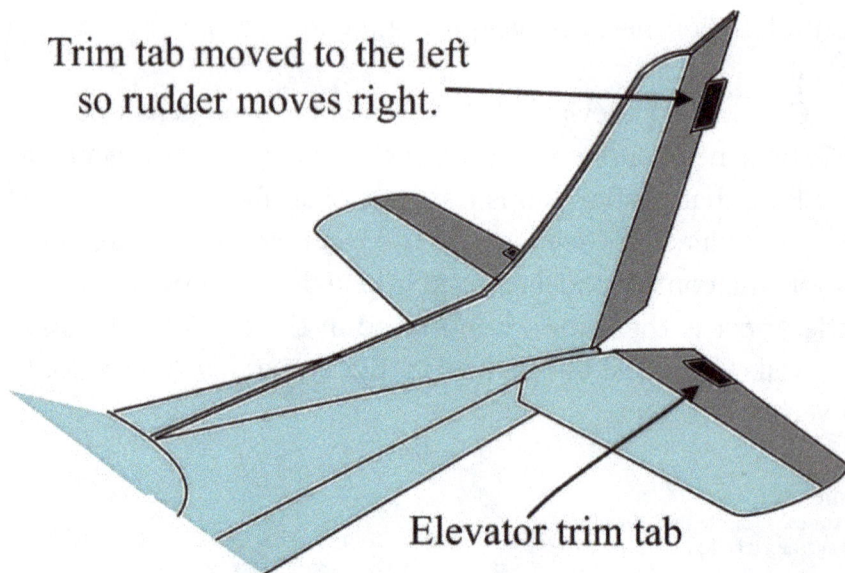

Fig 50. Trim tabs can be fitted to control surfaces

Differential ailerons

Differential ailerons simply means that the ailerons are linked
in such a way that the down aileron moves slightly less than
the up aileron and this evens out the difference in drag and
reduces adverse yaw. A designer at de Havilland invented a
simple linkage and the de Havilland Tiger Moth was the first
aircraft to use differential ailerons.

Frise ailerons

Frise ailerons have a shaped leading edge. The down aileron
has the top of the leading edge shaped to maintain the smooth
flow of air helping to keep down drag, while the up aileron also
projects slightly below the wing increasing drag, Fig 51. The

increase in drag on the down going wing counteracts the increased drag on the up going wing and so helps eliminate adverse yaw.

Down aileron maintains smooth airflow

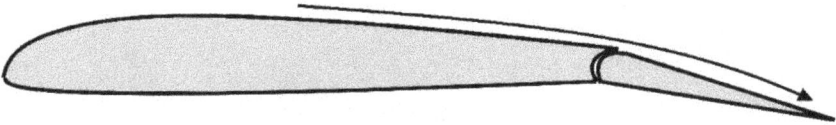

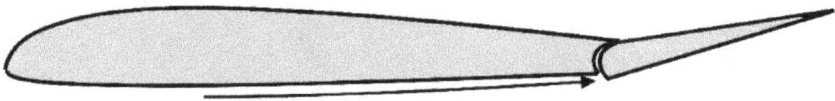

Up aileron projects below wing and causes increased drag

Frise Aileron

Fig 51. The up aileron projects below the wing and causes increased drag

Slots

Slots are designed to create a narrowing gap at the leading edge so that the airflow picks up speed, as in a venturi tube, and increases lift. The gap is really the slot, the small auxiliary aerofoil which forms the top surface is called a slat, Fig 52. Slots increase the lift generated by the wing, especially at large angles of attack and if we have slots, then the lowering of the aileron on the outer wing will be less likely to cause a stall and thus the lift will increase with only a very small increase in drag.

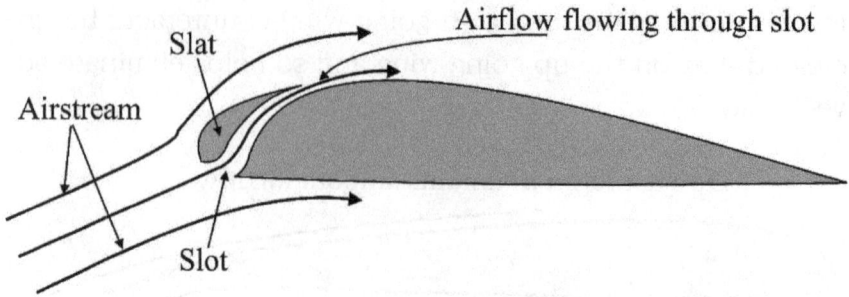

Fig 52

Spoilers

A spoiler (sometimes called a lift spoiler or lift dumper) is a device intended to intentionally reduce the lift component of an aerofoil in a controlled way. Most often, spoilers are plates on the top surface of a wing that can be extended upward into the airflow to spoil it. When deployed, the spoiler creates a controlled stall over the portion of the wing behind it, greatly reducing the lift of that wing section. Spoilers differ from airbrakes in that airbrakes are designed to increase drag without affecting lift, while spoilers reduce lift as well as increasing drag, Fig 53.

Spoilers fall into two categories: those that are deployed at controlled angles during flight to increase the rate of descent or control roll, and those that are fully deployed immediately on landing to greatly reduce lift (lift dumpers) and increase drag. In modern fly-by-wire aircraft, the same set of control surfaces is used for both functions.

Spoilers being deployed on an
airliner's wing in flight

Air brakes deployed on a glider
during final approach

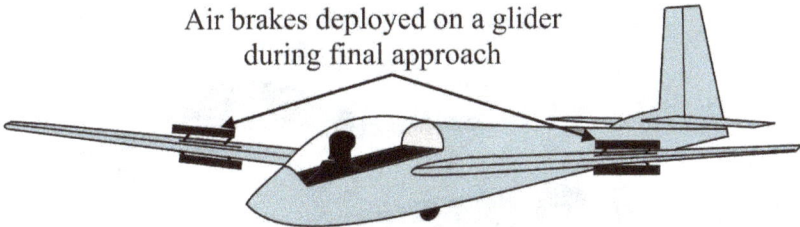

Fig 51. Spoilers on top of wing surface only but glider airbrakes open on top
and bottom surfaces

Airliners are almost always fitted with spoilers and they are used to increase the rate of descent without increasing speed. Their use is often limited, however, as the turbulent airflow that develops behind them causes noise and vibration, which may cause discomfort to passengers.

Spoilers may also be differentially operated for roll control instead of ailerons. However, the real gain comes as the spoilers cause a dramatic loss of lift and hence the weight of the aircraft is transferred from the wings to the undercarriage, allowing the wheels to be mechanically braked with less tendency to skid.

Helicopters

Wait a minute! I hear you cry, what about helicopters? You haven't mentioned them at all. Well I'll tell you what I know, firstly they use exactly the same aerofoil technology as aeroplanes, it's just that the aerofoils, or more properly, the rotors on a helicopter, instead of being fixed to the sides of the aircraft and thrust forward through the air to generate lift, rotate to generate the required airflow over the surfaces to generate the lift. So, just like the aerofoils of an aeroplane, the rotors have a leading and a trailing edge and therefore an angle of attack, Fig 54.

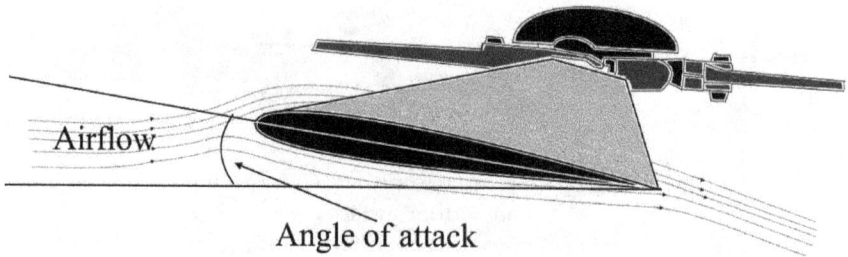

Airflow

Angle of attack

Fig 54

Now of course the tendency is for the helicopter, once it leaves the ground, to rotate in the opposite direction to the rotors and if that was allowed to happen, we would just end up with a rather dizzy pilot. The way to stop this counter-rotation is to equip the aircraft with a tail rotor, essentially a propeller, to keep the tail from rotating, Fig 55.

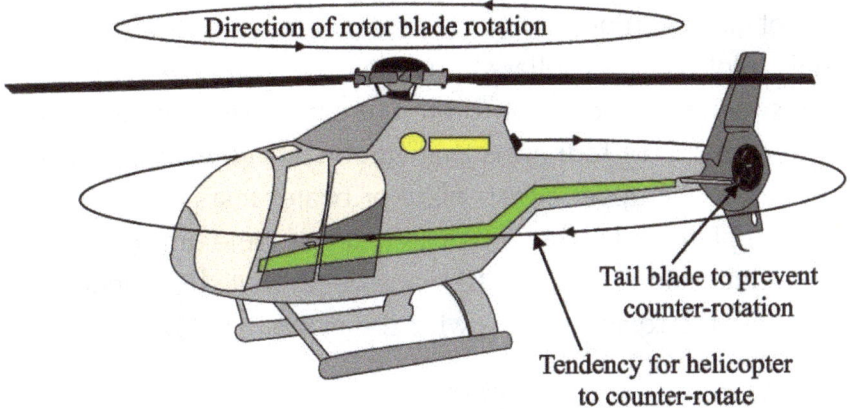

Direction of rotor blade rotation

Tail blade to prevent
counter-rotation

Tendency for helicopter
to counter-rotate

Fig 55

The Collective:

In order to control our helicopter, it is necessary for the pilot to be able to alter the angle of attack of the rotor blades and he can do this by using a control called the collective or (collective pitch,) which increases or decreases the angle of attack or "pitch" that all the blades present to the oncoming air as they rotate. If the amount of lift generated is greater than the weight of the aircraft it will rise in the air, if it is equal to the weight the aircraft will hover and so on. The collective control is normally situated to the left of the pilot's seat, rather like the handbrake on a car and it is called the collective because it alters the pitch of each rotor blade by the same amount.

The Cyclic Pitch:

Also known as the cyclic stick or just cyclic, the control is similar to the control column or joystick in a conventional fixed wing aeroplane and it also controls the pitch of the rotor blades but in a different way. The cyclic alters the pitch of the blades as they rotate or cycle around the rotor shaft by use of an ingenious piece of engineering. Around the rotor shaft itself are two collars known as "swash plates". The bottom swash plate does not rotate but can be tilted in any direction by means of four arms that can be moved up and down as required. The upper swash plate or bearer rests on top of the bottom plate and is therefore tilted at the same time and in the same direction as it, the difference being that this upper plate is connected to and rotates with the rotors, see Fig 56.

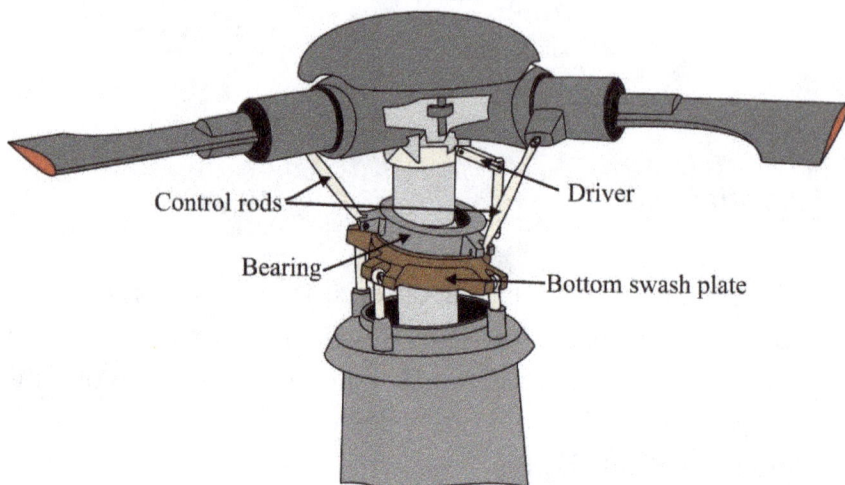

Fig 56

The upper plate has arms each of which are connected to the trailing edge of a rotor blade. In this way the pitch of each blade is altered as it rotates, allowing the pilot to generate more or less lift around the helicopter as required. For instance, if the pilot wants to bank his aircraft to the left, he will use the cyclic to lift the swash plate to the right, as shown, so that as the blades rotate on the right side of the aircraft, the control rods will pull the trailing edge down creating a greater angle of attack that side and generate more lift on the right, banking the helicopter to the left.

Anti-torque pedals:

The pilot can point the nose of his aircraft in any direction he chooses with the use of a pair of foot controls known as the anti-torque pedals, which alter the pitch of the tail rotor blades so they create more or less thrust that in normal straight flight. This makes the entire craft rotate clockwise or anti-clockwise as required by the pilot. The anti-torque pedals are located in the same place as the rudder pedals in a light aeroplane and perform pretty much the same task of yawing the aircraft. On tandem rotor helicopters like the Chinook, which do not require a tail rotor, the foot pedals tilt the swash plates in opposite ways, steering the aircraft accordingly. Fig 57 shows the layout of a typical helicopter cockpit.

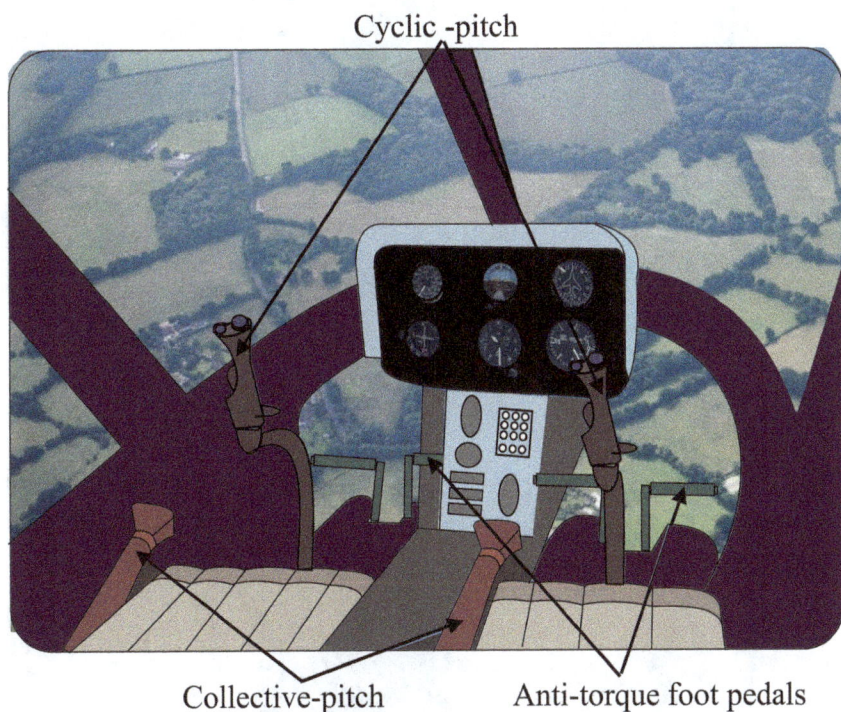

Fg 57. Helicopter cockpit layout

High Speed Flight

Darren Harbar Photography

Chapter 6

High Speed Flight

High Speed Flight

We have looked at how the control surfaces of an aircraft affect its attitude and how in some circumstances the pilot needs a little assistance moving them against the force of the airflow over them, and that has been at relatively low speeds. At high speeds the control surfaces can be difficult to move and are likely to be too effective or even too violent in action and so the controls on fast aircraft have to be both geared and power assisted.

We need our aircraft to have a range of speeds at which it can fly, fast for getting from place to place and slow, maybe for reconnaissance work and certainly for landing, so let us now consider how an aeroplane can stay in straight and level flight at different speeds and why its speed range is limited.

The determining factor is that lift must equal weight. In order to fly as fast as possible, the pilot decreases the angle of attack and increases the thrust until, because drag increases with speed, even with full power he can no longer maintain level flight, at which time he has reached the aircraft's maximum speed. In order to fly as slowly as possible, the pilot will increase the angle of attack and, counterintuitively, because drag increases with the angle of attack, once again he will increase the thrust until even with full power he can no longer maintain level flight, at which time he has reached the aircraft's minimum flying speed. This difference or ratio between the maximum and minimum speeds is the *speed range* of the aircraft.

Throughout the history of flight, attempts have been made to extend the speed range of aircraft and huge advances have been made but these advances have largely been in increasing the maximum speed to such a degree that fighter jets are now capable of traveling at over twice the speed of sound. This has largely come at the expense of slow flight, because if you ignore aircraft with vertical take-off capability, increases in maximum speed have also meant increases in minimum speeds.

The Sound Barrier

When we talked about the venturi tube and how draughts usually shut doors rather than open them, we discovered that air speeded up to go through a gap rather than compress and how this speeding up of the airflow reduced the air pressure. This tendency for air to speed up rather than compress is however, only true at speeds slower than the speed of sound.

Sound is in fact, no more than a pressure wave traveling through the air, if you make a noise of any kind, maybe by clapping your hands, the air is rapidly compressed and the pressure wave travels out from the source in all directions until it enters your ear, at which time you ear-drum vibrates and you hear the sound. Under normal atmospheric conditions sound travels at about 1,100 feet per second or as near as makes no difference, 760 miles per hour. This means that if something is traveling towards you at 760 miles per hour you will not hear it coming. If a man points a gun at you and you hear him fire it, you can take some comfort from the knowledge that he has missed you, because the bullet travels faster than sound and will have already passed you by the time the soundwaves reach your ear.

When an aeroplane travels through the air at speed less than the speed of sound the pressure waves created are able to travel ahead of it, as well as in other directions, and "warn" the air ahead of it that the aeroplane is coming and also that there is high pressure below the wing and low pressure above, so it is easier for the air to go above. Fig 58 shows how air that you might think would pass under the wing is warned by the pressure wave and is drawn up over the top of the wing.

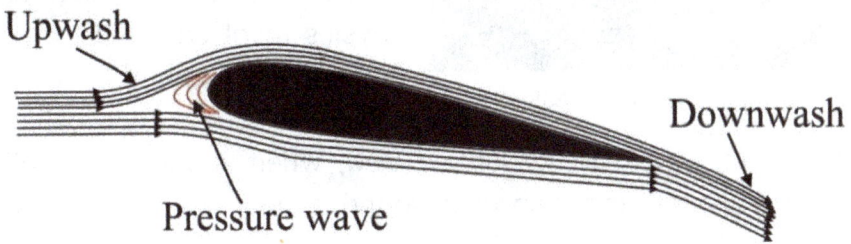

Upwash

Downwash

Pressure wave

Fig 58

If the aeroplane is travelling at the speed of sound, then the air in front will get no advanced warning of it and the air, instead of being deflected in time, will come up against it with a sudden shock, and that is in effect, the sound barrier.

This phenomenon was predicted by Ernst Waldfried Josef Wenzel Mach towards the end of the nineteenth century, Fig 58A.

Fig 58A. Ernst Mach (1838-1916)

Mach's early work focused on the Doppler effect in optics and acoustics but in 1864 he took a job as Professor of Mathematics at the University of Graz, having turned down the position of a chair in surgery at the University of Salzburg to do so, and in 1866 he was appointed as Professor of Physics.

His main contribution to physics involved his description and photographs of spark shock-waves and then ballistic shock-waves. He described how, when a bullet or shell moved faster than the speed of sound, it created a compression of air in front of it. Fig 58B.

Using schlieren photography, he and his son Ludwig were able to photograph the shadows of the invisible shock waves.

(*Schlieren photography is a visual process that is used to photograph the flow of fluids of varying density and is widely used in aeronautical engineering to photograph the flow of air around objects.*)

During the early 1890s Ludwig was able to invent an interferometer which allowed for much clearer photographs.

The speed of sound is, as you can see, a very significant speed in aviation and for that reason we often talk of how fast an aeroplane is travelling, not in terms of miles per hour, but to how fast it is going compared to the speed of sound, its Mach Number. So, if an aeroplane is travelling at the speed of sound, we say it is travelling at Mach 1, or if it is travelling at half the speed of sound, at Mach 0.5 and one and a half times, Mach 1.5 and so on.

Now you may ask why we do this, if the speed of sound is 760 miles per hour, why not just use that speed? The answer to that question is because, if you look back to where I stated the speed, I said that it was 760 miles per hour, *under normal atmospheric conditions*, that's because the speed that sound travels in air depends upon the atmospheric conditions that exist at the time, most importantly the air temperature.

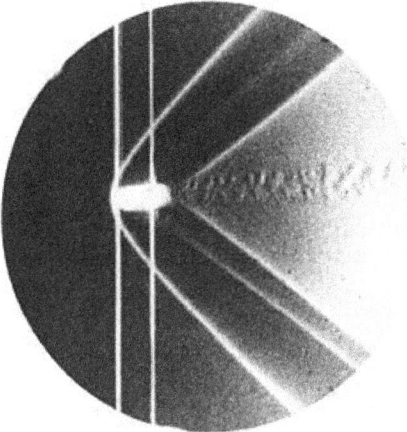

Fig 58B. Ernst Mach's 1887 photograph of a bow shockwave around a supersonic bullet

At ground level, under conditions of the International Standard Atmosphere, the speed of sound is about 760 miles per hour, while in the stratosphere (above 37.000 ft.) it is about 660 m.p.h. so an aeroplane travelling at 700 m.p.h. may be below the speed of sound, at the speed of sound or above the speed of sound, according to the temperature of the air. Normally, we do not need to know the exact Mach number that an aeroplane is travelling at, only whether it is below, at, or above the speed of sound so it is more convenient to use the Latin words and speak of subsonic, sonic and supersonic speeds.

Shock Waves

We know that when we approach the speed of sound the air is no longer warned of our approach and it comes as a sudden shock. The evidence for this is the appearance of a shock wave, a sharp dividing line going out from the surface of the body or wing and representing a sudden drop in the speed and an increase in the pressure and density of the air, Fig 59.

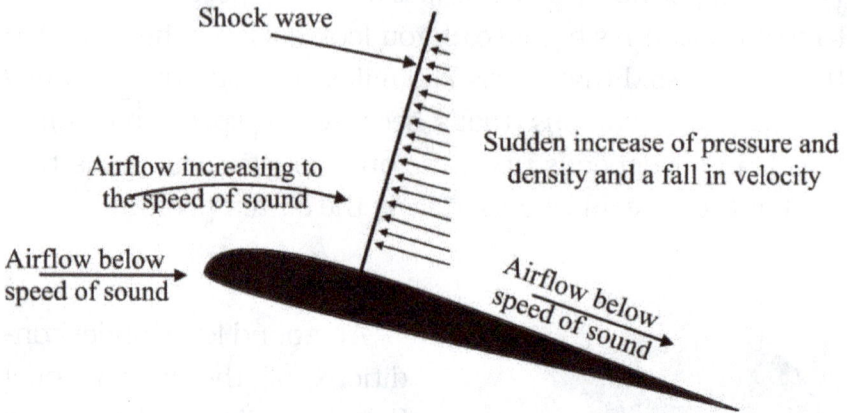

Shock wave

Airflow increasing to the speed of sound

Sudden increase of pressure and density and a fall in velocity

Airflow below speed of sound

Airflow below speed of sound

Fig 59 A shock wave

These shock waves are not usually visible to the human eye but sometimes a vapour cone is visible, this happens when the air temperature drops below the saturation point temperature as the aircraft breaks the sound barrier, Fig 60.

Fig 60. Vapour cone as aircraft breaks the sound barrier. Courtesy of Realbigtaco (CC BY-SA 3.0)

The effect of the shock wave is quite dramatic and the air near the surface of the wing behind the shock wave becomes violently turbulent and the whole distribution of pressure over the wing is changed, resulting in loss of lift and an increase in drag rather like a stall with all the associated buffeting and shaking and loss of control. The effect is so much like an ordinary stall in fact, that it is called a shock stall, Fig 61.

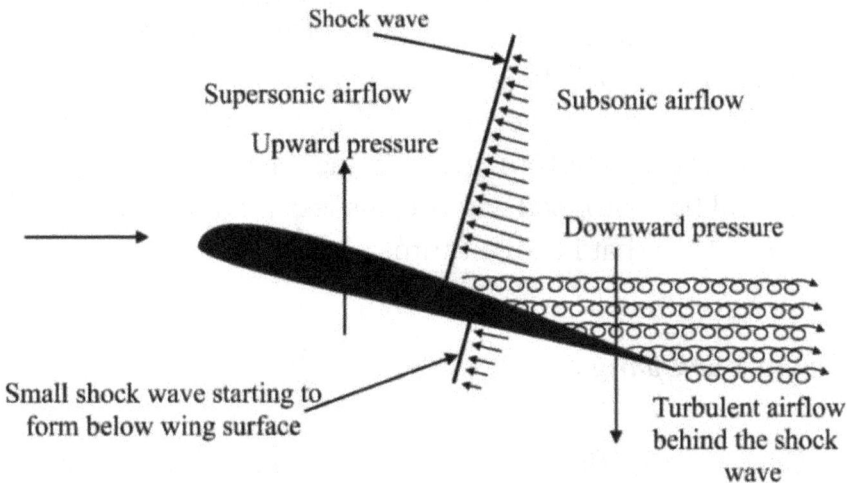

Fig 61. The shock stall

There are some differences however, in an ordinary stall the controls become sloppy and ineffective, whereas in a shock stall they become stiff and difficult to move. The main difference however, is that an ordinary stall occurs at a large angle of attack or very low speed, a shock stall is obviously at high speed and can occur at any angle of attack. To recover from an ordinary stall, we must put the nose down and increase speed, but to recover from a shock stall we must reduce speed by either pulling the nose up or by using some kind of air brake.

The shock wave, when it occurs, also causes a new kind if drag called "wave drag" that first appears at the shock stall and at the same time, the sudden rise of pressure in the shock wave upsets the flow of air in the boundary layer, causing it to separate from the surface and become turbulent over the remainder of the surface. This is yet another source of drag called "boundary layer" or "separation drag".

Before the sound barrier was broken it was thought that the ordinary stall and the shock stall were the limits to flight. If you flew too slowly you would stall and similarly, if you flew too fast you would stall. Now the difference in speeds between the two was quite big at low level in normal conditions, say around 100 m.p.h. for a normal stall and 700 m.p.h. for a shock stall but at 40,000 ft. the ordinary stalling speed of 100 m.p.h. becomes 200 m.p.h. due to the fall in density of the air and even higher in a tight turn. At the same time the shock stalling speed will have dropped and become less than 600 m.p.h. and even less than that in a tight turn.

Swept back wings

Once the significance of the shock stall had been realised the designers set to work, they knew that slimness was a way of reducing drag and that they needed a wing with a low ratio of thickness to chord and a laminar flow aerofoil but their most important contribution was the introduction of the swept back wing.

Now we discovered earlier that the airflow over the top surface of the wing is speeded up because of the shape of the wing, this means that even before the aircraft itself is traveling at the speed of sound, the airflow over some part of it will be and this will cause a shock wave. The Mach number at which this occurs is known as the Mach number of the aeroplane. The more cambered the wing the more likely it is that the airflow somewhere will exceed the speed of sound and so the lower will be the critical Mach number. It is clearly an advantage therefore, to have a slim wing with a high critical Mach number, so that the aircraft can get as close to the speed of sound without experiencing a local shock stall.

The speed of airflow over a swept back wing can be thought of as having two components, that which flows across the chord, that is at right angles to the leading edge, and that which flows along the span of the wing towards the wing-tip parallel to the leading edge, Fig 62.

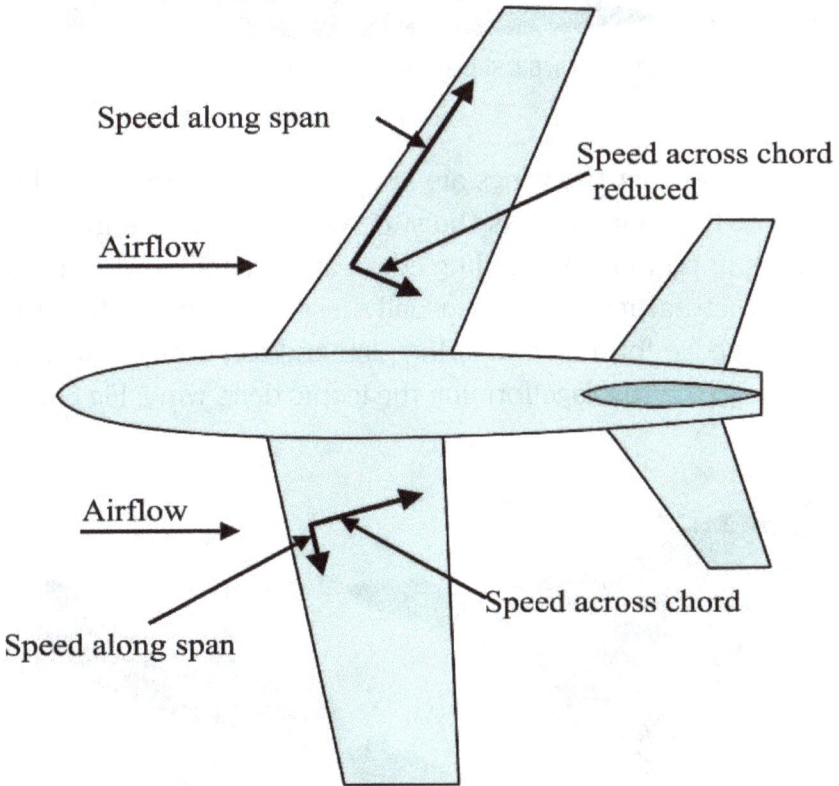

FIg 62. The more swept back the wing the more the airspeed across the chord is reduced in relation to the aircraft's speed

Now the greater the sweep back of the wing, the more the speed of the airflow across the chord is reduced in comparison to the speed of the aircraft as a whole, so the nearer we can get to the speed of sound without experiencing a shock stall.

So, the section through an aerofoil designed for supersonic flight is going to be different to one designed for subsonic flight, it's going to be thinner, have less difference in the camber top and bottom and be more symmetrical in the fore and aft section, Fig 63.

Leading edge **Trailing edge**

Fig 63. Supersonic wing section

The fact that the wings are swept back will affect the plan view of the wing but it is the sweep back of the leading edge that is important, the trailing edge can be parallel with it but for structural reasons it is usually less swept back than the leading edge forming a tapering plan and can even be at right angles to the fuselage forming the iconic delta wing, Fig 64.

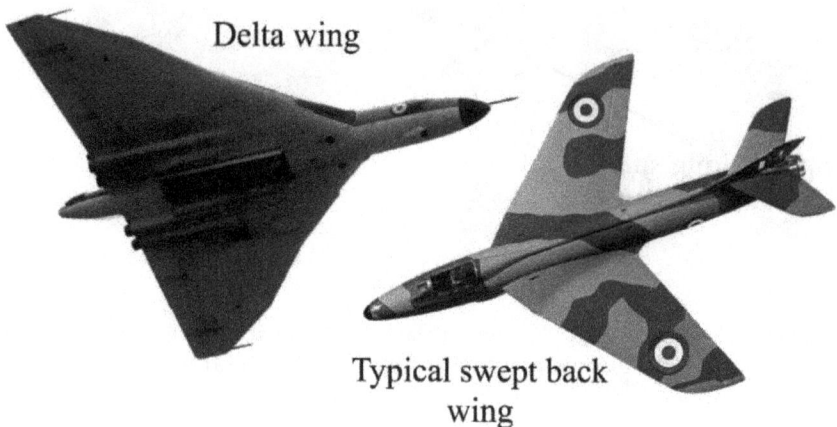

Delta wing

Typical swept back wing

Fig 64. It's only the leading edge that needs to be swept back.

Supersonic flight

The sound barrier is not of course a real barrier, because the term barrier implies that it is impossible to cross and we have known for a long time that wasn't the case. A bullet from a gun travels faster than sound and the "crack" that you hear when you crack a whip is not the sound of the tip hitting anything, it is the tip of the whip breaking the sound barrier and producing a mini sonic boom. The sound barrier is better described as a hurdle that has to be passed and once we are on the other side things become easier, *different* but easier. It is the crossing over from subsonic to supersonic speeds, the transonic stage, that is so difficult, the speed between Mach 0.75 and Mach 1.2 with all the associated changes in drag and lift and the formation of shock waves.

Fig 65 gives some idea of these changes in diagram form. First a small shock wave appears on the upper surface at about the highest point of the camber, where the air is flowing fastest. As the Mach number increases the shock wave becomes more intense, it extends further from the aerofoil and moves backwards, at which time another shock wave begins to form a little further back on the bottom surface. As speed increases still further the shock wave becomes fully developed and continues to move back until it reaches the trailing edge.

Soon after the whole of the wing is traveling supersonic, at Mach numbers greater than 1.0, (D in Fig 65), another shock wave appears ahead of the leading edge. After this, further increases in speed have little effect on the shock wave except that it takes up a more acute angle and the bow wave may become attached to the leading edge. These are indications that the whole airflow over the wing is now supersonic.

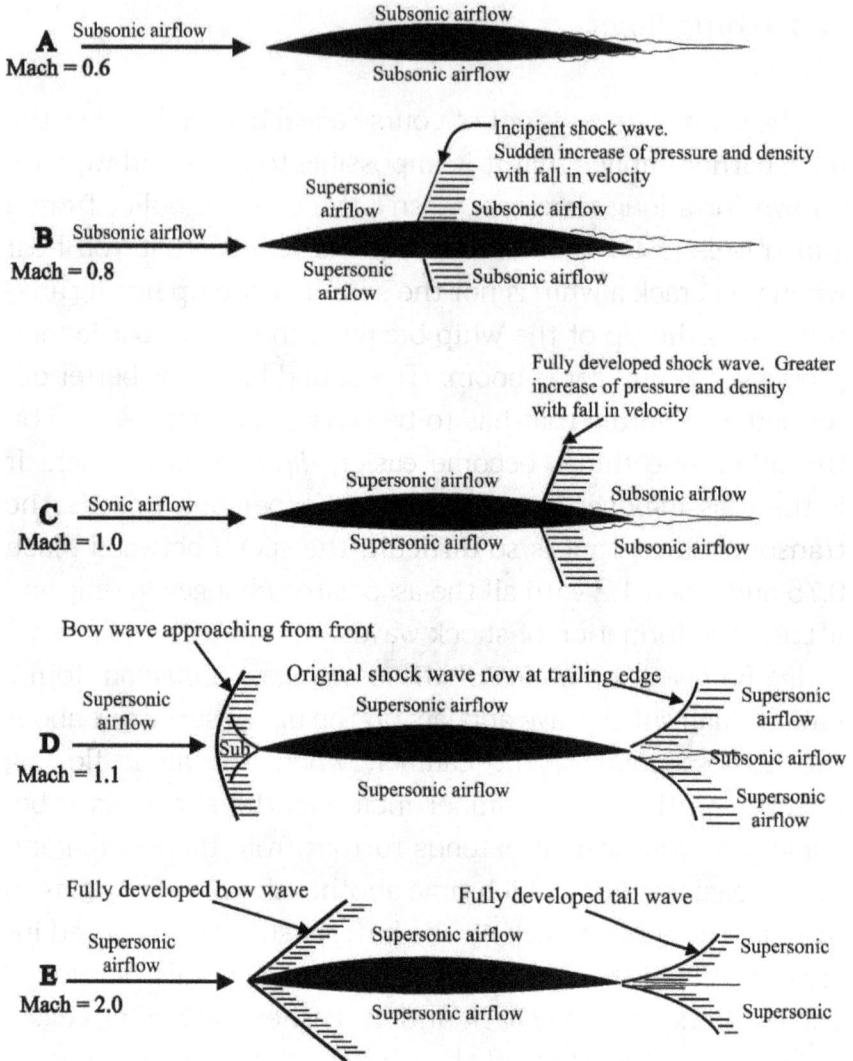

A Subsonic airflow
Mach = 0.6

Subsonic airflow
Subsonic airflow
Subsonic airflow

Incipient shock wave.
Sudden increase of pressure and density
with fall in velocity

Supersonic
airflow
Subsonic airflow

B Subsonic airflow
Mach = 0.8

Supersonic
airflow
Subsonic airflow

Fully developed shock wave. Greater
increase of pressure and density
with fall in velocity

Supersonic airflow

C Sonic airflow
Mach = 1.0

Supersonic airflow

Subsonic airflow
Subsonic airflow

Bow wave approaching from front

Original shock wave now at trailing edge

Supersonic
airflow

Supersonic airflow

Supersonic
airflow

D
Mach = 1.1

Sub

Subsonic airflow

Supersonic airflow

Supersonic
airflow

Fully developed bow wave

Fully developed tail wave

Supersonic
airflow

Supersonic airflow

Supersonic

E
Mach = 2.0

Supersonic airflow

Supersonic

Fig 65. Trasonic stages of flight

A Whole New World

Once we emerge on the other side of the sound barrier and leave transonic speeds behind us things become smooth again, it turns out that it was only when we were in a world of some subsonic and some supersonic airflow that things got nasty.

However, our new world is quite different to our old one, we are now in a world of compressibility, where airflow likes to meet sharp pointed objects rather than the smoothly rounded ones of subsonic airflow.

Here, in the supersonic world, air entering a venturi tube dislikes the narrowing duct and instead of speeding up to flow through nicely, it produces shock waves, the air slows down and the pressure increases, the complete opposite in fact of what happens with subsonic flow.

On the other side of the venturi tube, where the duct opens up and where subsonic airflow slowed down and pressure increased, supersonic airflow speeds up and pressure drops off. In both cases however, a speeding up of airflow goes with a drop in pressure. Chalk one up for Bernoulli's Theorem.

So, a supersonic Venturi Tube would be the reverse of a subsonic one, Fig 66.

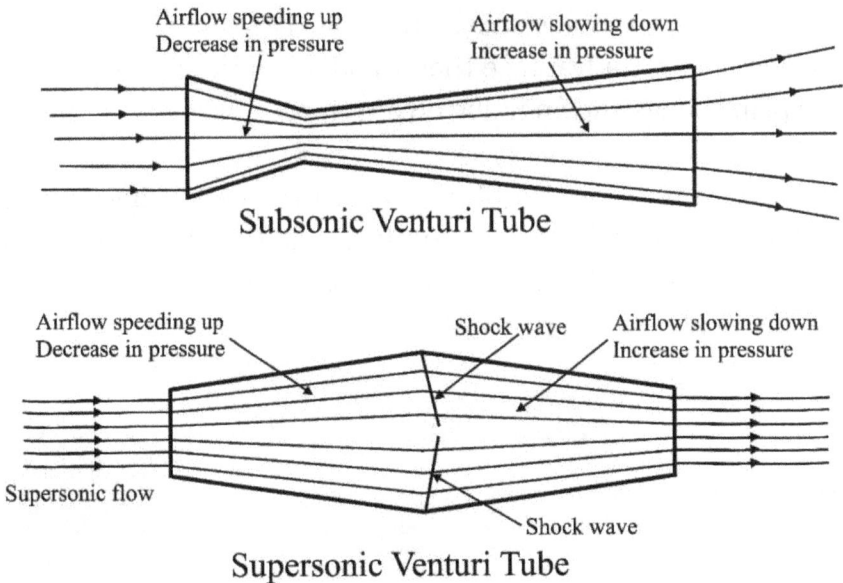

Airflow speeding up
Decrease in pressure

Airflow slowing down
Increase in pressure

Subsonic Venturi Tube

Airflow speeding up
Decrease in pressure

Shock wave

Airflow slowing down
Increase in pressure

Supersonic flow

Shock wave

Supersonic Venturi Tube

Fig 66

The way the supersonic airflow reacts to the supersonic Venturi Tube also accounts for the shapes of aerofoils that are designed for supersonic speeds, some of which are illustrated in Fig 67.

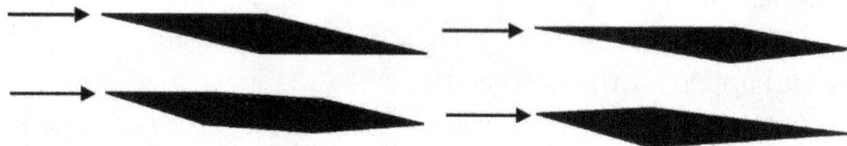

Fig 67. Supersonic aerofoil shapes

However, although in subsonic flight it is the cross-section shape of the wing that is more important than the plan shape, in supersonic flight the plan is more important than the cross-section.

At lower supersonic speeds the heavily swept back leading edge retains the advantage that it had at transonic speeds and the plan shapes shown in Fig 68 are all possible.

You can see from Fig 68 that although the leading edge is swept back to one degree or another in all the plan views, this is not the case for the trailing edge which can in some cases be at right angles to the fuselage.

Fig 68

Forward swept wings

I should note here that some aircraft actually have a forward sweep to the wings rather than a backward one. Airflow over a swept wing tends to flow spanwise towards the back end of the wing. This flow is towards the wing tip on a conventional backward swept wing but is towards the fuselage on a forward swept one, Fig 69.

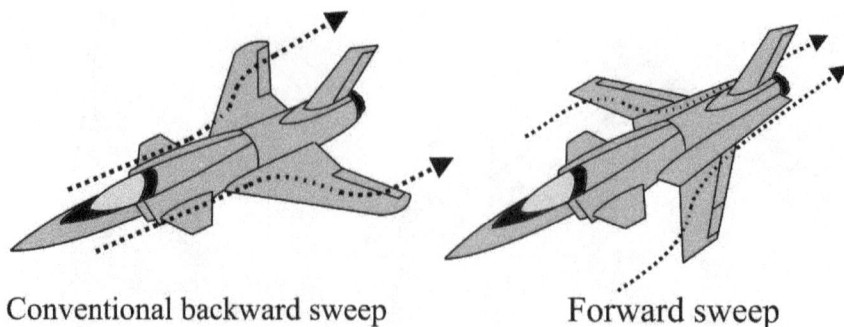

Conventional backward sweep   Forward sweep

Fig 69. Airflow over forward and backward swept wings

As a result, the dangerous wing tip stall condition of a rearward-swept design becomes a safer and more controllable root stall on a forward-swept design. This allows full aileron control despite loss of lift. With the air flowing inwards, wingtip vortices and the accompanying drag are reduced. Instead, the fuselage acts as a very large wing fence, (a device designed to prevent some of the spanwise airflow towards the wing tip.) and, since wings are generally larger at the root, this raises the maximum lift coefficient allowing a smaller wing. As a result, manoeuvrability is improved, especially at high angles of attack and at transonic speeds, shockwaves build up first at the root rather than the tip, again helping to ensure effective aileron control. An example of an aircraft with it's wings swept forward is shown in Fig 70.

In the years leading up to Chuck Yeager becoming the first person to break the sound barrier in level flight on October 14, 1947 we began to understand more about the so called "sound barrier" and what we needed to do to cross it. The introduction of swept wings was a huge leap forward in the design of high-speed aircraft, as was Otto Frenzi's discovery in 1943 of the "Area Rule".

Fig 70. A Grumman X-29. Courtesy of NASA/JPL-Caltech.

The area rule says that two airplanes with the same longitudinal cross-sectional area distribution have the same wave drag, independent of how the area is distributed laterally (i.e. in the fuselage or in the wing). Furthermore, to avoid the formation of strong shock waves, this total area distribution must be smooth.

Richard T. Whitman experimented with various shapes in a wind tunnel in 1952. He discovered that the addition of wings to a simple cylinder produced twice as much drag as the cylinder alone. He also found that drag increased by the same amount if a simple bulge, the same equivalent volume as the wings, were added instead. However, if he reduced the cross-sectional area of the cylinder at the site where the wings were attached, the drag was about the same as that for the cylinder alone, Fig 71.

As a result, aircraft have to be designed so that, at the location of the wing, the fuselage is narrowed or "waisted", so that the total area doesn't change very much, a classic example of which is the F-106 Delta Dart shown here in Fig 72.

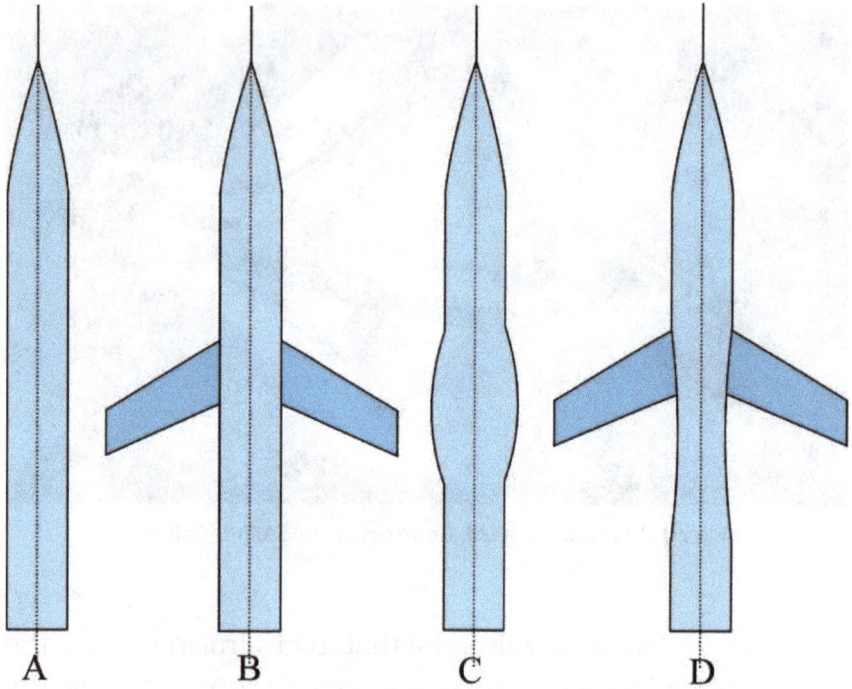

Fig 71

A   Cylindrical fuselage alone
B   Addition of wings doubled the amount of drag
C   Bulged fuselage produced same amount of drag as the addition of wings
D   Waisted fuselage with wings produced no more drag than fuselage alone

Similar but less pronounced fuselage waisting is used at the location of a bubble canopy and perhaps the tail surfaces. The area rule also holds true at speeds exceeding the speed of sound but in this case the "perfect shape" is biased rearward; therefore, aircraft designed for high speed cruise usually have wings located towards the rear.

Fig 72, F-106 Delta Dart showing waisting. NASA photograph by Jim Ross: (creative commons licence)

So, we come to the end of this section of the book, have I covered everything? Nowhere near, but hopefully I have done what I set out to do and that is to explain in simple terms just how an aeroplane can fly.

Now, a great many people have contributed to our knowledge of flight over the years and before I finish this book I would just like to mention a couple of them in the next chapter.

Early Pioneers

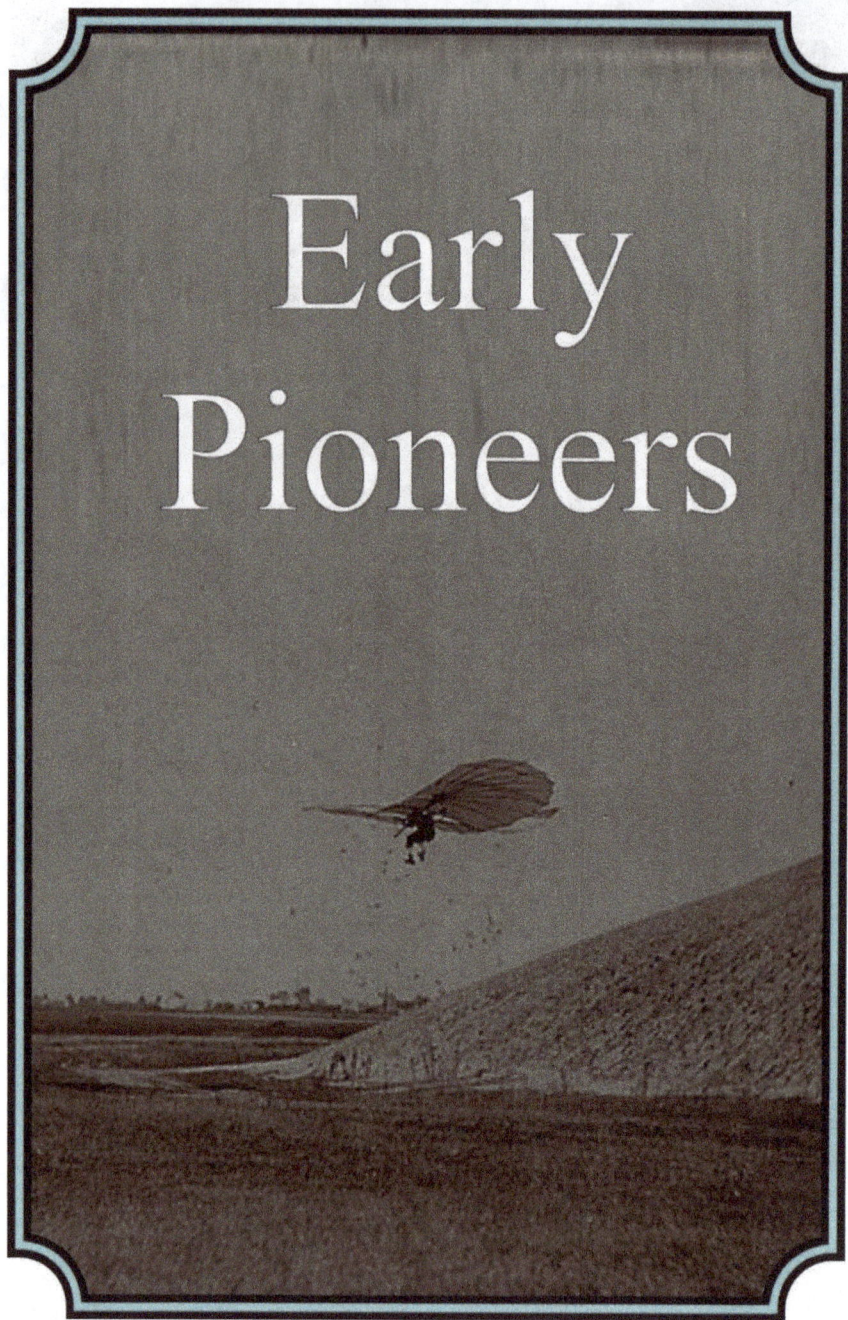

Chapter 7

Some Pioneers of Flight

George Cayley (1773-1857)

George Cayley (1773 – 1857)

In China, the earliest known flying toys consisted of feathers at the end of a stick, which was rapidly spun between the hands and released into flight. "While the Chinese top was no more than a toy, it is perhaps the first tangible device of what we may understand as a helicopter and it was the object of early experiments by George Cayley.

In 1792, he began experimenting with helicopter toys, which he later called "rotary wafts" or "elevating fliers," and in his landmark article of

1809 "On Aerial Navigation" he pictured and described a flying model with two propellers (constructed from corks and feathers) powered by a whalebone bow drill. In 1835 Cayley remarked that while the original toy would rise no more than about 20 or 25 feet (6 or 7.5 metres,) his improved models would mount upward of 90 ft (27 metres) into the air. This then was the direct ancestor of the helicopter rotor and the aircraft propeller.

George Cayley identified the four forces involved in heavier than air flight, weight, lift, drag and thrust but must have been frustrated at the time by the lack of a powerful or light enough engine, so he concentrated his efforts on gliders, a sketch of one his model gliders, drawn by Cayley himself, is shown here.

His full-size glider had a large wing attached to a pole, at the rear of which was a horizontal tailplane and a vertical rudder and when anyone ran forward with it at full speed, Cayley stated that it would *frequently lift them into the air and convey them several yards together*". Cayley's calculations of lift and drag and his observations on stability and control of an aeroplane in flight were a solid base on which progress could be made but for some reason, progress stalled for some thirty years.

George Cayley's drawing of a glider

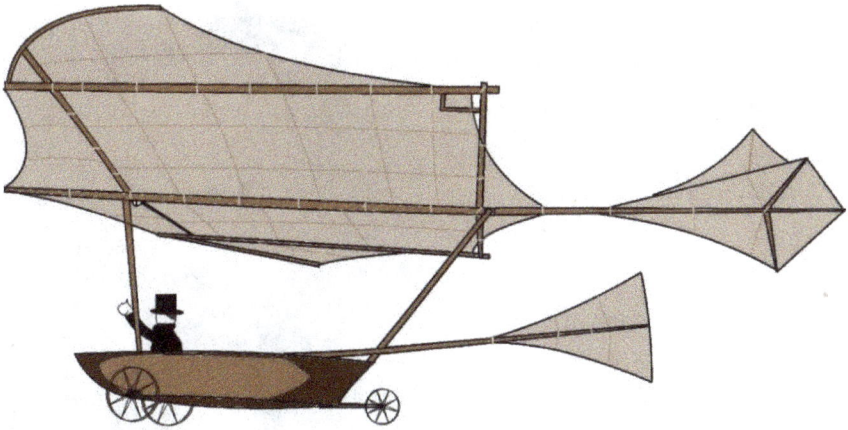

An impression of George Cayleys full-size glider.

Henson and Stringfellow

William Samuel Henson (1812-1888)

Two names stand out when it comes to steam powered flight, John Stringfellow, (1799 – 1883) and William Samuel Henson (1812 – 1888,) both man are remembered for their work on the Aerial Steam Carriage, illustrated here. The two men, who both worked in Chard, in Somerset, England, had visions of creating the Aerial Transit Company and designed an elaborate passenger carrying aircraft, the design stage was as far as it got however, but nevertheless, it was the first in history for a propeller-driven fixed-wing aircraft.

At first Henson managed to attract potential investors for his proposed company with his elaborate drawings of his carriage flying in exotic locations but in the end, he failed to persuade anyone to put up the necessary money for a full size aircraft and the project was abandoned.

In 1848 John Stringfellow achieved the first powered flight using an unmanned, steam-powered monoplane

John Stringfellow (1799-1883)

with a 10ft wingspan. It was built in a disused lace factory in Chard, Somerset and employed two opposite hand propellers.

On the first attempt, made indoors, the machine flew ten feet before becoming destabilised, damaging the craft. The second attempt was more successful however, the machine, following a guide wire to start with for stability, flew freely after release for some thirty yards of straight and level powered flight. A bronze model of that first primitive aircraft stands in Fore Street in Chard.

In 1866 the Aeronautical Society of Great Britain was founded and in 1888 they held their first aeronautical exhibition and awarded John Stringfellow a £100 prize for his invention of a steam engine with the best power-to-weight ratio.

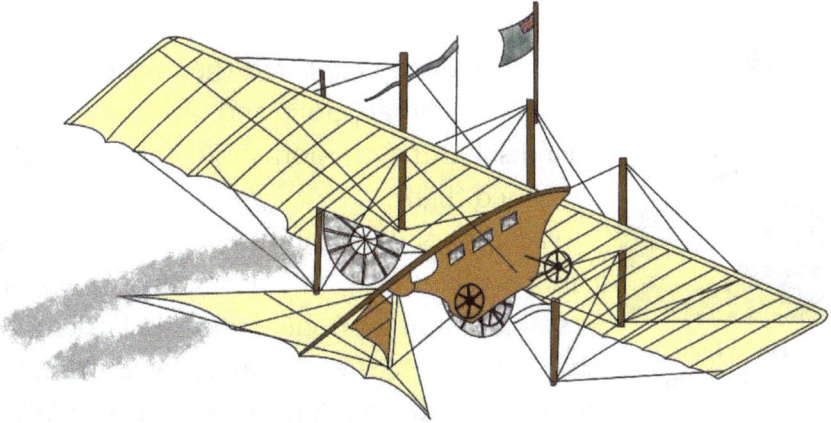

Henson and Stringfellow's idea for an Aerial Steam Carriage

A replica of John Stringfellow's successful aeroplane

Karl Wilhelm Otto Lilienthal (1848 – 1896)

Karl Wilhelm Otto Lilienthal was a German aviator who became known as the "flying man," and was the first person to make well-documented, repeated, successful flights with gliders. Lilienthal became something of a celebrity at the time, with newspapers and magazines publishing photographs of him gliding.

**Karl Otto Lilienthal
(1848-1896)**

This publicity captured the imagination of the wider general public and favourably influenced scientific opinion about the possibility of maned flight.

His gliders were carefully designed to distribute weight as evenly as possible to ensure a stable flight and he controlled them by changing the centre of gravity by shifting his body, much like modern hang gliders today.

However, they were difficult to manoeuvre and had a tendency to pitch down, from which it was difficult to recover, the reason for which was that he held the glider by his shoulders, rather than hanging from it like a modern hang glider. Only his legs and

Lillienthal flying a biplane glider

lower body could be moved and this limited the amount of weight he could move.

Lillienthal bout to fly a monoplane glider

In 1894 he filed a U.S. patent that directed pilots to grip the bar of an A-frame for carrying and flying the glider that sounds very much like the control frame of modern hang-gliders. With his brother Gustav Lilienthal, he made over 2,000 flights in gliders, until on 9th August 1896, the glider he was flying stalled and he was unable to regain control. Falling from about 15 m (50 ft), he broke his neck on landing and died the next day, 10th August 1896.

The Wright Brothers

Wilbur Wright (1867-19120)

Wilbur and Orvile Wright are generally accepted as having guilt the world's first, heavier than air aeroplane to accomplish a manned, sustained and controlled powere flight. It happened on the 17th December 1903 four miles south of Kitty Hak, North Carolina and in 1904-05 they developed their machine into the first practical fixed wing aircraft, the Wright Flyer 111.

The brothers' breakthrough came with their creation of a three-axis control system which enabled the pilot to steer the aircraft effectively and to maintain its equilibrium. From the beginning of their aeronautical work, the Wright brothers had focused on developing a reliable method of pilot control as the key to achieving pow-

Orville Wright (1871-1948)

ered flight, whereas most others had concentrated more on developing more powerful engines. Their first patent for example, was not for a flying machine but for a system of aerodynamic control that manipulated a flying machine's surfaces.

The Wright Flyer 111

In December 1892 the brothers, capitalising on the development of the safety cycle and the increased popularity of cycling, opened a cycle repair and sales shop "the Wright Cycle Exchange," and in 1896 they began manufacturing their own brand of cycle.

They used the profits from this business endeavour to fund their growing interest in flight and in the early or mid-1890s they read newspaper or magazine articles about the dramatic glides that had been performed by Otto Lilienthal in Germany.

There were several events in 1896 that captured the interest of the brothers, Samuel Langley's successful flight of an unmanned steam powered model, Octave Chanute's glider flights and the tragic death of Karl Wilhelm Otto Lilienthal. The brothers later said that it was with the death of Otto Lilienthal that their interest in flight research really began, drawing on the work of Cayley, Langley, Lilienthal and Chanute.

Wilbur wright had noted, after observing birds in flight, that they changed the angle of the ends of their wings to make their bodies roll right or left.

The brothers decided this would also be a good way for a flying machine to turn, to bank or lean into the turn just like a bird, and just like a person riding a bicycle, an experience with which they were thoroughly familiar. Equally important, they hoped this method would enable recovery when the wind tilted the machine to one side, thus restoring "lateral balance."

They puzzled over how to achieve the same effect with man-made wings and eventually discovered wing-warping, illustrated here, when Wilbur idly twisted a long inner-tube box at their bicycle shop.

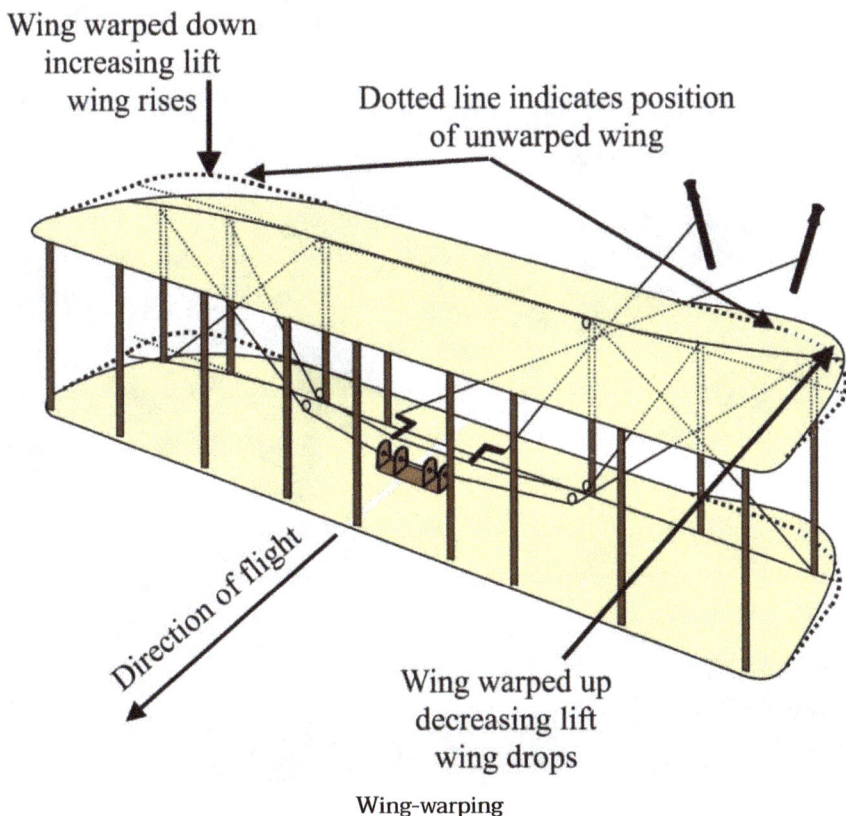

Wing warped down
increasing lift
wing rises

Dotted line indicates position
of unwarped wing

Direction of flight

Wing warped up
decreasing lift
wing drops

Wing-warping

Most designers at this time envisaged aircraft as steering in much the same way as other craft, like trains and boats, they thought a rudder would do the steering while the aeroplane stayed level in the air, the idea of deliberately rolling to one side in order to turn seemed both dangerous and unnecessary. In 1899 the brothers built a biplane kite with wing warping capability; the warp being controlled by four cords attached to the kite and operated by the kite flyer.

The Wright brothers based the design of their kite and full-size gliders on work done in the 1890s by other aviation pioneers. They adopted the basic design of the Chanute-Herring biplane hang glider or the "double-decker" as the Wrights called it, which had flown well in the 1896 experiments near Chicago, and they used the aeronautical data on lift that Otto Lilienthal had published.

The Wright brother's kite

The brothers designed the wings of their plane with camber, a curvature of the top surface. They had not been the the first ones to discover this principle and it's advantage over a flat one, it first being discussed by Sir George Cayley, but they took advantage of it. Lilienthal, whose work the Wrights had carefully studied, also used cambered wings in his gliders, proving its advantage over flat ones in actual flight.

The wooden uprights between the wings of the Wright glider were braced by wires and was their own version of Chanute's modified Pratt truss, a bridge-building design he used for his biplane glider. They mounted their horizontal elevator in front of the wings rather than behind, apparently believing this feature would help to avoid or at least protect them from a nosedive and crash, like the one that had killed Lilienthal. Wilbur however, incorrectly believed a tail was unnecessary and their first two gliders did not have one.

Wilbur lay flat on the lower wing, as planned, in order to reduce aerodynamic drag and as a glide ended, he was supposed to lower himself into a vertical position through an opening in the lower wing and land on his feet with his arms wrapped over the framework. Within a few glides, however, they discovered that he could remain prone on the wing without undue danger when landing and they made all their subsequent flights in that position for the next five years.

In 1902, their third glider, after a few modifications, did use a trailing rudder for yaw and it responded well to the controls. They initially used wing warping to control roll and a forward elevator for pitch. The glider, however, delivered two major disappointments. It produced only about one-third the lift calculated and sometimes pointed opposite to the intended direction of a turn when Wilbur used the wing-warping control, a problem later to become known as adverse yaw. On the trip home, a deeply dejected Wilbur remarked to Orville that man would not fly in a thousand years.

Wilbur, just having landed their 1901 glider

The poor lift experienced with the gliders led the Wrights to question the accuracy of Lilienthal's data, as well as the "Smeaton coefficient" of air pressure, a value which had been in use for over 100 years and was part of the accepted equation for lift. *(In 1759, John Smeaton, (1724 – 1792) an English civil engineer, had published a paper entitled, "An Experimental Enquiry Concerning the Natural Powers of Water and Wind to Turn Mills and Other Machines Depending on Circular Motion")*. Smeaton developed the concepts and data which became the basis for the Smeaton coefficient,the lift equation used by the Wright brothers.

It has the form:

L = kV2 ACl   where:
                      L is the lift
                      k is the Smeaton coefficient
                      V2 is the velocity squared
                      A is the area in square feet
                      Cl is the lift coefficient (the lift relative to
the drag of a plate of the same area)

To learn whether errors existed in Lilienthal's data tables, the brothers used one of their bicycles for a new type of experiment. They made a model-sized aerofoil and a counter-acting flat plate, both according to dimensions Lilienthal had specified, and attached them to an extra bicycle wheel, which they mounted horizontally in front of the handlebars, an illustration of which is shown here.

Pedalling strenuously on a local street to create airflow over the apparatus, they observed that the third wheel rotated against the aerofoil instead of remaining motionless as Lilienthal's formula predicted. The experiment confirmed their suspicion that either the standard Smeaton coefficient or Lilienthal's coefficients of lift and drag or both of them—were in error.

The brothers then built a six-foot (1.8m) wind tunnel in their workshop and between October and December 1901 they conducted systematic tests on dozens of model wings. The "balances" they devised and mounted inside the tunnel to hold the wings may have looked crude, made of bicycle spokes and scrap metal, but they were as critical to the ultimate success of the Wright brothers, as were the gliders.

Initial conditions

Model wing   Drag plate

s = spoke length
b = angle

b   b

Test conditions

Wind

Lift
L   A = rotation angle

a

b + a   b - a

Drag
D

$$L \sin(b+a) = D \cos(b-a)$$

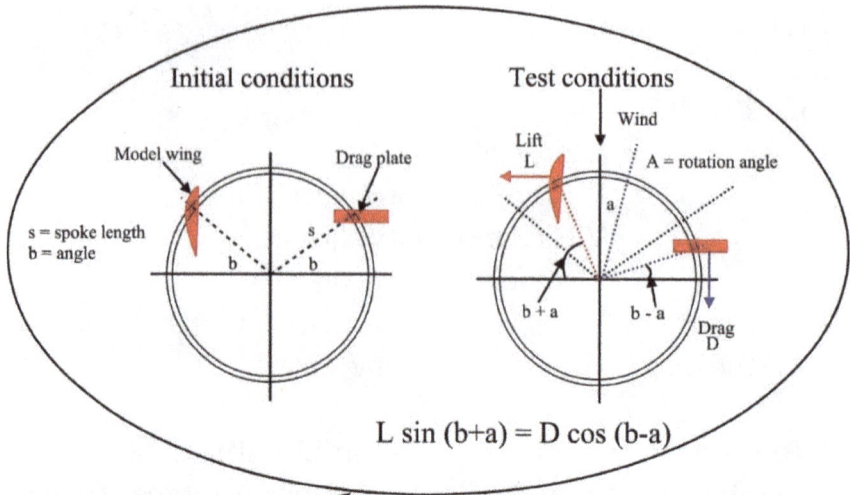

The Wright brother's bicycle wheel experiment

The devices allowed the brothers to balance lift against drag and accurately calculate the performance of each wing. They could also see which wings worked well as they looked through the viewing window in the top of the tunnel. The tests provided them with a huge amount of valuable new data and showed that the poor lift of the 1900 and 1901 gliders was almost entirely due to an incorrect Smeaton value. They also established that Lilienthal's published data was fairly accurate for the tests he had done.

Over the years a wide variety of values had previously been measured for the Smeaton coefficient; Chanute identified some of them and Wilbur knew that Langley had used a lower number than the traditional one. Determined to confirm the correct Smeaton value, Wilbur performed his own calculations using measurements collected during kite and free flights of the 1901 glider. His results correctly showed that the coefficient was very close to 0.0033 (similar to the number Langley had used), not the traditional 0.0054, which would significantly exaggerate predicted lift.

The 1902 glider flown as a kite

With typical caution, the brothers first flew their 1902 glider as a kite, the same as they had done with previous tests, and using the newly obtained figures, the 1902 glider flew at a much flatter angle of attack and held up its tether lines almost vertically, and thus clearly demonstrating a much better lift to drag ratio.

It was also in 1902 that they realised that it was the wing warping that caused the aircraft to turn away from the direction of bank, (adverse yaw). Increasing lift on one wing also increased the drag causing the front of the aircraft to point away from the direction of turn. It was for that reason that they incorporated a rear steerable double rudder to counteract the adverse yaw. In short, it was the Wright brothers that discovered that the real purpose of a rear steerable rudder, was not to change the direction of travel, as the rudder on a boat, but rather to align the aircraft correctly during a banking turn and eliminate adverse yaw. The actual turn was achieved by banking the aircraft with wing warping, and later with ailerons.

Their new glider with its steerable rudder performed so well that they were able to make numerous successful flights and it was the foundation of three axis control, wing warping for bank or roll, a forward sited elevator for pitch and a steerable rear rudder for yaw control, all they needed to do was add power and the true aeroplane had arrived.

They built their "Wright Flyer" from spruce and covered it in muslin, after which they looked for a suitable propeller and engine. They wrote to several engine manufacturers, but none could meet their need for a sufficiently lightweight engine, so they enlisted the help of their shop mechanic.

In the end, the wright brothers built their own 12 hp, four-cylinder engine in eight weeks with the aid of Charles Taylor, their shop mechanic and machinist, but without drawings. The engine weighed 170 lbs. including the radiator, water and fuel tanks, and 1.5 gallons of petrol. With no throttle, the four-stroke engine always ran at about 1,000 rpm. but output could be somewhat controlled by retarding or advancing the spark timing.

The crankcase, cylinder water jacket, mounting lugs, and part of the intake manifold were cast as a single piece of aluminum and because it was hand-made, there were no interchangeable parts, each piston for example, only fitted the cylinder it was made for.

The Wright brother's engine

The valves were of the poppet type and the camshaft was driven by a bicycle chain from their workshop. The fuel was gravity fed into the intake manifold where it was vaporized by the hot water jacket and sucked through the inlet valve and into the cylinders. The engine needed to be overhauled after every twelve hours of use.

There were no established design formulae for either a marine or an air propeller at that time so they set about designing and carving their own. Working on the assumption that a propeller was simply an aerofoil mounted vertically, they used wind tunnel tests to design one and they ended up with a propeller that was over eight feet long and later discovered to be 66% efficient. They decided to use two counter-rotating propellers in order to cancel out torque and to transfer power from the engine to the propellers they devised a simple chain and sprocket arrangement running from the engine crankshaft to a pair of steel propeller shafts. To make the propellers rotate in opposite directions they simple twisted one of the two chains into a figure of eight.

At Kill Devil Hills, they endured weeks of delays caused by broken propeller shafts during engine tests and after the shafts were replaced, a process that required two trips back to Dayton, Wilbur won a coin-toss and made a three-second flight attempt on December 12th 1903, stalling after take-off and causing minor damage to the Flyer. December 13th 1903, was a Sunday so the brothers didn't make any attempts that day, even though the weather was good, so their first powered test flight happened on the 14th December 1903.

In a message to their family, Wilbur referred to the trial as having *"only partial success"*, stating *"the power is ample, and but for a trifling error due to lack of experience with this machine and this method of starting, the machine would undoubtedly have flown beautifully."*

Following repairs, the Wright brothers finally took to the air on December 17th 1903, making two flights, each from level ground into a freezing headwind gusting to 27 miles per hour (43 km/h). The first flight, by Orville at 10:35 am, of 120 feet (37 m) in 12 seconds, at a speed of only 6.8 miles per hour (10.9 km/h) over the ground, was recorded in a now famous photograph shown below.

Orville takes off for the first flight with Wilbur running beside

The next two flights covered approximately 175 and 200 feet (53 and 61 m), by Wilbur and Orville respectively. Their altitude was about 10 feet (3.0 m) above the ground. The following is Orville Wright's account of the final flight of the day:

"Wilbur started the fourth and last flight at just about 12 o'clock. The first few hundred feet were up and down, as before, but by the time three hundred ft had been covered, the machine was under much better control. The course for the next four or five hundred feet had but little undulation. However, when out about eight hundred feet the machine began pitching again, and, in one of its darts downward, struck the ground. The distance

*over the ground was measured to be 852 feet; the time of the
flight was 59 seconds. The frame supporting the front rudder
was badly broken, but the main part of the machine was not injured at all. We estimated that the machine could be put in condition for flight again in about a day or two."*

Five people witnessed the flights: Adam Etheridge, John T.
Daniels, who snapped the famous "first flight" photo using
Orville's pre-positioned camera, Will Dough, all of the U.S. government coastal lifesaving crew; area businessman W.C. Brink-
ley; and Johnny Moore, a teenaged boy who lived in the area.
After the men hauled the Flyer back from its fourth flight,
a powerful gust of wind flipped it over several times despite
the crew's attempts to hold it down. Severely damaged, the
aeroplane never flew again. The brothers shipped it home, and
years later Orville restored it and lent it to several U.S. mu-
seums and institutions for display, then to a British museum,
before it was finally installed in 1948 in the Smithsonian Insti-
tution in Washington, D.C. where it currently resides.

In 1904 they built the Wright Flyer 11 and began slowly
withdrawing from their cycle business to concentrate on mar-
keting a practical aeroplane, a brave decision owing to the fact
that they were not rich by any means and had no government
backing. For this reason, they became much more secretive
about their work on the advice of their patent attorney Henry
Toulmin.

After several crashes in Flyer 11, Wilbur finally made the
first ever complete circular flight in history by a manned heav-
ier-than-air powered machine, covering 4,080 feet (1,244 m) in
about a minute and a half. Eventually they scrapped the now
somewhat battered and bruised Flyer 11 but kept the engine
and built a new craft, the Flyer 111, shown earlier.

After Wilbur suffered a near fatal crash on 14[th]July 1905,
they rebuilt the machine with the forward elevator and rear

rudder both enlarged and placed several feet further away from the wings. They also installed a separate control for the rear rudder instead of linking it to the wing-warping cradle as before. Each of the three axes, pitch, roll and yaw, now had its own independent control and these modifications greatly improved stability and control, enabling a series of six long flights ranging from 17 to 38 minutes and 11 to 24 miles (39 km) around the three-quarter mile course over Huffman Prairie between September 26th and October 5th.

Wilbur made the last and longest flight, 24.5 miles (39.4 km) in 38 minutes and 3 seconds, ending with a safe landing when the fuel ran out. The flight was seen by a number of people, including several invited friends, their father Milton, and neighbouring farmers.

Despite these remarkable events, and possibly due to their own secrecy surrounding their test flights, there was a great deal of scepticism about their achievements in both the American press and in Europe.

The Wright brothers didn't make any flights at all in 1906 or 1907, instead spending their time trying to persuade the U.S. and European governments that they had indeed invented a successful flying machine and that they were prepared to negotiate a contract to sell such machines. They also experimented with a pontoon and engine setup on the Miami River (Ohio) in hopes of flying from the water but these experiments proved unsuccessful. Disappointed that the American government appeared unimpressed they turned their attention to France where there was great enthusiasm for aviation and also to Britain and Germany where they met aviation representatives who were impressed with the Model A Flyer that they had shipped over.

On returning to the U.S. they found that the U.S. Board of Ordnance in Washington had had a change of heart. Both America and France now wanted them to bid for contracts and both contracts required them to give public demonstrations and to carry a passenger. To comply with the contracts, they modified their 1905 Flyer by adding two seats and upright control levers.

After several tests with sandbags in the passenger seat, Charlie Furnas, a helper from Dayton, became the first fixed-wing aircraft passenger in a few short flights on 14th May 1908. For safety, and as a promise to their father, Wilbur and Orville never flew together but several newspaper reporters at the time mistakenly took Orville's flight with Furnas as both brothers flying together. Later that day, after flying solo for seven minutes, Wilbur suffered his worst ever crash when, still not well-acquainted with the two new control levers, he apparently moved one the wrong way and slammed the Flyer into the sand at between 40 and 50 miles per hour. Luckily, he emerged with only bruises and a cut nose, but the accident ended both the practice flights and that aeroplane's flying career.

On August 8th 1908, Wilbur Wright made his first flight in public at the Hunaudieres race course, five miles south of Le Mans, France and over the next several weeks he made headlines around the world with one stunning flight after another, demonstrating once and for all that the Wrights' claim to priority in the invention of the aeroplane was true and that their aeroplanes were capable of tight turns and a degree of control not possible with other machines.

Orville Wright joined his brother in the limelight on September 3rd 1908, when he made his first public flight at Fort Myer, Virginia. Tragedy struck however on September 17th when Orville crashed at Fort Myer while flying with Thomas Etholen Selfridge, a first lieutenant in the U. S. Army, as a passenger. Three or four minutes into the flight, a blade on one of the two wooden propellers split and caused the engine to shake violently.

Orville shut down the engine but was unable to control the aeroplane. The propeller had hit a bracing wire and pulled a rear rudder from its vertical position to a horizontal one causing the aeroplane to pitch nose-down and rendering control impossible.

The Wright Flyer hit the ground hard, and both men were injured. Orville suffered a fractured leg and several broken ribs but the unfortunate Thomas Selfridge suffered a fractured skull and a few hours later, he became the first person to die in a powered aeroplane crash. Orville recovered, but lived with the pain resulting from the accident for the rest of his life.

Once Orville Wright was back on his feet, he and his sister Katharine joined their brother in Europe. The three Wrights were now the toast of the continent. Crowned heads, political leaders, captains of industry and ordinary folk travelled to witness the miracle of flight. Wilbur capped off this extraordinary year with a flight of more than 76 miles in 2 hours 18 minutes 33 seconds on December 31st which earned him the Michelin Cup and a 20,000-franc cash prize for the best flight of 1908.

In the Summer of 1909, the Wright brothers arrived home to find they had become celebrities in America as well as Europe. They were treated to an endless series of awards and honours, including a city-wide homecoming celebration in Dayton, Ohio. They spent what little spare time they could find building a new Military Flyer. In the summer they took their new aeroplane back to Fort Myer, Virginia and completed the trials that had been interrupted almost a year earlier and the U.S. Army purchased its first military aircraft for $30,000.

Henri Coandă

The Coandă-1910, designed by Romanian inventor Henri Coandă was an unconventional sesquiplane aircraft powered by a ducted fan. Called the "turbo-propulsor" by Coandă himself, its engine consisted of a conventional piston engine driving a multi-bladed centrifugal blower which exhausted into a duct. The strange arrangement attracted a lot of attention at the Second International Aeronautical Exhibition in Paris in October 1910, presumably because it was the only exhibit without a propeller. The aeroplane does not appear to have been shown anywhere else but Coandă used a similar turbo-propulsion engine to drive a snow sledge, although he did abandon the idea for aircraft.

An impression of the Coandă turbo-propulsor 1910

He discovered the Coandă effect in fluid dynamics and invented a great number of devices, he also designed a "flying saucer" employing the Coandă effect.

Between 1911 and 1914, he worked as technical manager of the Bristol Aeroplane Company at Filton in the United Kingdom, where he designed several aeroplanes known as the Bristol-Coanda Monoplanes. In 1912 one of these aircraft won a prize in the British Military Aeroplane Competition.

INDEX

Other books by Colin Holcombe

The Story of Flight   (hardback)
ISBN: 978-1-5272-6762-6

The Story of Flight   (paperback)
ISBN: 978-1-675480601

A History of Firearms
ISBN: 978 1987591453

Samuel Colt. The Man Behind the Gun
ISBN: 978 1787234031

Cabinet Making
ISBN: 978 1787233393

Antique Furniture Restoration an Illustrated Guide
ISBN: 978 1787233522

The Care and Repair of Antique Furniture
ISBN: 978 1516899081

www.ingramcontent.com/pod-product-compliance
Lightning Source LLC
Chambersburg PA
CBHW050218270326
41914CB00003BA/462